Breakthrough strategies to supercharge your business and earn loyal customers for life

by

Howard Brodsky

with Dustin S. Klein

A Smart Business Network Inc. imprint

Published by:
Smart Business Network
835 Sharon Dr., Suite 200
Westlake, OH 44145

Printed in the United States of America

Editor: Randy Wood
Cover design: Kaelyn Hrabak
Interior design: Randy Wood

ISBN: 978-0-9889622-9-3

Library of Congress Control Number: 2013954242

Contents

Dedication

To my sons, Jeff and Greg, for their guidance, friendship and love.

HB

To Laura, Sam, Cole and Mollie.

With love, DSK

Part One

The Unexpected

1 The Unexpected In A Predictable World

Back in 2006, colleagues and I were traveling from Boston to Long Beach, California, to attend a company conference for our organization, CCA Global Partners. There were about 100 of us, so we traveled in two groups of about 50 people each. One group flew out in the morning; the other in the afternoon. We were flying on JetBlue, and I was in the first group.

About an hour into the flight, the pilot came on the intercom. He said that we had encountered a 200 mph headwind, which was slowing us down. And, because the plane was full, the pilot explained that it would be impossible to reach Long Beach without stopping to refuel.

Air traffic control rerouted us to Minneapolis-St. Paul International Airport, he explained, where we would land, refuel and then resume our flight to California. What we expected would be a six-hour trip now would take us about nine hours.

Because JetBlue doesn't provide meals on its flights, I had packed a light lunch. But that wasn't nearly enough food to last a nine-hour flight. I realized we were all going to be a lot hungrier when we got to California than I'd originally thought. So I settled in for a longer than expected day.

A few moments later, the pilot came back on the intercom.

"Folks," he said. "I feel bad about all of this, so I'm going to give all of you a $25 gift certificate and a free movie. We'll do what we can to make sure the remainder of your flight with us is uneventful. Thank you for choosing JetBlue, and we hope you'll decide to do so again."

This, in my opinion, was the definition of world-class customer service. The pilot — and the airlines — had no obligation to go above and beyond giving us the gift certificate. It wasn't JetBlue's fault that Mother Nature had disrupted the flight. Still, the pilot was empathic to our plight, and despite the inconvenience, we all felt pretty good about how JetBlue was treating us.

Later that day, after we arrived in California, reached our hotel and settled in for the conference, the second group of travelers from CCA Global Partners arrived. Stories about their experience started circulating. And their story was almost beyond belief.

The second group boarded their JetBlue flight in the afternoon and ran into similar weather. They flew into the same 200 mph headwinds we had and were unable to reach Long Beach nonstop. Their plane was re-routed to Denver for refueling.

And that's where the stories' similarities ended.

When our second group reached Long Beach that evening and reconnected with the rest of our company, it didn't take long for those 50 people to spread their story of what happened in Denver to the more than 3,000 people in attendance at the conference.

According to my colleagues on the second plane, shortly before landing in Denver, the intercom system sprang to life.

"This is the captain speaking. Once again, we apologize for this delay," the pilot said. "I've been thinking about this. If I was in your position, expecting it to be a six-hour flight and finding out it would now be a nine-hour flight, I'd be starving.

"I go to Denver quite a bit," the pilot continued. "There's a Pizza Hut about two miles from the airport. So I personally arranged for a call to the

Pizza Hut and ordered 25 large pizzas. They will be delivered to the plane on the tarmac, along with a number of side items. I thought you might like this. We'll let you know when they arrive. On behalf of the entire crew here at JetBlue, thank you for your continued patience."

As the story goes, the entire plane burst into applause.

While the pizza delivery didn't do much to speed up the wait, the announcement by the pilot — and subsequent delivery of the pizzas to the plane — was so unexpected that it changed the tenor of everyone on the plane. They went from feeling disappointment, maybe even anger over the delay, to elation that something so thoughtful was being done for them.

> Customers are looking for meaningful connections. Those organizations that provide them gain a competitive advantage.

Buying the pizzas probably didn't cost the crew much, perhaps a few hundred dollars to feed every person on the plane. In fact, that was significantly less than the cost incurred by JetBlue for the $25 gift certificates distributed on my flight.

This wasn't about the money spent. It was about delivering thoughtful service to customers; specifically, JetBlue's ability to deliver unexpected service to its customers by empowering its front-line employees to think creatively, to do whatever it takes to turn any situation into a positive experience — without the need to secure approval from anyone higher up the chain of command.

JetBlue's management team — already recognized as having built a forward-thinking organization that consistently delivered world-class customer service — realized that just being consistently great wasn't enough. And so they ensured every member of their employee team was capable of going one step beyond.

By creating an experience that became legendary for those who were there, JetBlue transcended its own well-regarded reputation and further differentiated itself from its competitors.

It's likely that every person who was on our planes told at least one other person about what they experienced. And, in this viral society where social media has made it possible to instantly transmit information worldwide to thousands, if not hundreds of thousands of people, friends heard about this story within moments of the plane's landing. Each time, it probably began the same way: "You won't believe what happened to me on this JetBlue flight."

Three days later, *USA Today* picked up the story. It was national news; a new legend for JetBlue was born.

As an entrepreneur, the experience gave me an epiphany. I recognized immediately how special this was. This was the power of what I've deemed The Unexpected, another level of customer service that organizations deliver to separate themselves from others in their industries.

Since then, I have come to understand just how powerful a differentiator delivering The Unexpected can — and will — be for any organization. In fact, once you start applying it, The Unexpected just may become the most powerful tool in your business toolbox.

Today, business is more challenging than ever. Competition is ruthless, and it is ever increasing. We live in an environment where we almost have too much of everything, and our options for where we spend are money are nearly overwhelming. Learning to deliver The Unexpected will become a transformational experience for you, your employees and your industry. And, like any transformational experience, it will have broad-reaching impact.

I've come to believe we are standing on the cusp of a new chapter in business and the economy, and The Unexpected is a key driver of the change. It is a cluttered world out there. Everyone is fighting for attention. Those who develop ways to better engage with prospects, clients, vendors and employees will create separation from their competition. And the methods used will quickly become those organizations' secret sauce. Why shouldn't it be you and your organization? The Unexpected can be your way.

JetBlue, which has always been on the leading edge of world-class service, knew the importance of separation well. They grasped the idea that companies must take service to the next level and deliver The Unexpected in order to surprise clientele when they needed to be surprised the most.

But delivering The Unexpected isn't as easy as just deciding you're going to do something fun and interesting at a certain moment. It can't be a planned event. It can't be something written down on a card that says, "When X happens, do Y." Rather, it must be spontaneous and responsive. But it can be systematic.

The more I've studied The Unexpected, the more I realize what it takes to make it part of an organization's fabric.

My own organization, CCA Global Partners, is a large, multinational conglomerate holding company with 13 divisions and more than 2,700 locations. CCA Global Partners' companies employ thousands of people, each of whom brings their own personal service experiences to work every day.

We compete with such industry giants as Home Depot and Lowe's in our given segments. And when we do so, we must find ways to differentiate ourselves from those big-box competitors in order to win in the marketplace.

Because of my role, I have the honor to speak before groups of employees, other CEOs and entrepreneurs on a regular basis. I've previously served as the chairman of the national judging committee for the Retail Category for the EY Entrepreneur Of The Year™ Awards. And I've served as national judge for the EY Entrepreneurial Winning Women™ program, which is working to help connect, mentor and empower the fastest growing segment of business start-ups in the nation — women entrepreneurs. All of these have provided the unique experience to see firsthand what successful entrepreneurs do, how great businesses operate and what makes them so different from others in their industries.

A few common themes come to mind: First, world-class entrepreneurs have great passion for what they do. They are dreamers who want to change an industry and are doggedly determined to achieve their goals.

Second, they demonstrate a great tolerance for risk. In fact, their risk tolerance level is much higher than other people's, reminding me of the famous saying by Sir Winston Churchill, who claimed, "Success consists of going from failure to failure without loss of enthusiasm."

Third, great entrepreneurs recognize that in business there is no finish line. They are always on the hunt for what's next, constantly searching for ways to improve upon the status quo.

And finally, although I didn't really realize it until after the JetBlue experience, these entrepreneurs know that in order to be best-of-class they must deliver The Unexpected, not just provide great customer service.

It is this ability — understanding the difference between world-class customer service and The Unexpected — that has become so much more important than it was just years ago.

So beyond the JetBlue adventure what exactly is The Unexpected? And why do companies that deliver it separate themselves from a crowded pack?

To better understand, let's first look at what comprises world-class customer service.

In the hospitality industry, for example, you might check into a hotel as a traveler. The check-in desk clerk sees that you're part of the hotel's Great Travelers' VIP Club, so he tells you that he's going to give you a complementary room upgrade. The room is nice. It's clean. The maid service is really great. And so your stay is comfortable and you leave pleased that you received an upgrade and the experience was that much better. Better yet for the hotel chain, you'll most likely stay with them again.

But this isn't The Unexpected.

You signed up for this type of service. You've received upgrades before, most notably at airlines where you're a frequent flier, so this was more of a nice touch — getting more than you paid for — rather than a true surprise.

The Unexpected, on the other hand, becomes etched in your memory banks when it's delivered. That's because our brains react favorably to receiving it. Dopamine circuits fire, telling our brains to pay attention to what is happening and creating feelings of joy and happiness.

Think about the impact this has with instant communications through Twitter, LinkedIn and Facebook. If entire revolutions and citizen uprisings can be initiated through these mediums, imagine how powerful a positive, unexpected experience with your organization can be when your customers begin spreading the word because they're filled with happiness and joy?

Building and maintaining your brand suddenly takes on a life of its own; your clients spread the word about what a wonderful thing you did and start looking forward to what you might do next.

But delivering The Unexpected isn't limited to just your customers and vendors. In fact, by applying it internally, you'll create an equally powerful effect. Start putting surprises such as movie tickets or flowers on your employees' desks to recognize extra effort or special occasions. Offer pet insurance for your employees' pets. Provide free-lunch Mondays or Fridays. And, every once in a while, break up the workweek with a companywide luau, fiesta or ice cream social in the middle of a Wednesday afternoon.

Suddenly, your company's reputation will change. No longer will you be known as simply an above-average — or even great — organization that offers a competitive paycheck, merit raises and quality health insurance for its employees. Instead, you will rise to the next level and become a world-class employer of choice. Your candidate pools will become loaded with top talent as other companies' employees will look to you as the place they want to work and to yours as the team they long to join.

In a world where the war for talent has become fiercer, and where every company's survival depends on its ability to attract and retain top employees, using The Unexpected internally will help transform your business. And as a result, you will recruit better, dramatically increase employee retention and significantly reduce turnover.

Better yet, you don't need to implement anything that carries a high price tag in order to get people talking. And when they talk, the legend will grow.

Incorporating The Unexpected into your organization does come with a bit of caution, however. You can't plan a series of events for customers or employees, call them The Unexpected, and then hope that people take notice and start flocking to your doorstep. When you do the same thing again and again it becomes expected and you no longer separate yourself from your competition. Separating yourself permanently is what The Unexpected is all about.

> "The key is to set realistic customer expectations, and then not to just meet them, but to exceed them — preferably in unexpected and helpful ways."
> —Sir Richard Branson, founder, Virgin Group

The really great organizations, like JetBlue, empower the people on the front lines to use their own judgment and creativity to deliver The Unexpected. It cannot be a corporate mandate to do this or offer that. Instead, the mandate from the top is to empower employees to do whatever it takes to create lasting memories that clients will talk about.

I had the opportunity in 2012 to hear an amazing presentation from Christian Davies, the executive creative director of design firm Fitch, which underscored just how powerful delivering an unexpected experience for consumers can be when you combine visual and tactile surprise and delight.

If you're not familiar with them, Fitch has earned a reputation as the go-to firm worldwide for translating brand into customer experience. Davies' message was loud and clear: There is too much stuff out there.

He explained that information overload is clouding what people truly value. Consumers seek to free themselves of the noise and clutter they encounter daily, and they're looking for meaningful connections, especially emotional connections, with the organizations they do business with.

Davies described how Fitch understands this transformation and why The Unexpected plays such a crucial role in it.

Fitch creates distinguishable experiences for its customers, including Nike, Puma and HTC. They are memorable and personal experiences; the types of engagements consumers are unable to receive anywhere else.

Take for example Nike's hi-tech retail space at a posh London shopping center, Boxpark, which is made out of shipping containers.

Fitch worked with Nike to develop a space that would communicate the company's brand message and showcase a new product — the Nike+ FuelBand, a fitness band that tracks the wearer's movements and allocates points based on their activity levels.

"The latest shoes and sports clothing are displayed along the ways," Davies explained. "But with such limited space, touch screens are on hand to explore the whole product range."

This, however, isn't where The Unexpected comes in. That happens when consumers suddenly come face-to-face with the interactive technology.

"Stand in front of a mirror," Davies continued. "It turns into a screen showing a local fitness enthusiast describing their daily exercise regime."

And then, as if that weren't memorable enough, a Kinect-powered, motion-sensitive wall turns movement into pixels, which Davies says can be recorded and shared with friends via social media.

Nike's well-known culture of above-and-beyond customer service ties together the entire experience. For example, staff members are able to set up FuelBands for customers, use an in-store treadmill, and assess a customer's running style to better match him or her with the most suitable running shoes.

For Fitch, this is all part of its corporate mystique. For Davies, delivering The Unexpected means Fitch is developing the next great trend for its clients in each of their respective industries. It means staying retail-focused, thinking global, and ensuring every idea is actionable and scalable. As a result, every experience the company creates for its clients turn into stories that consumers can't help but recount over and over.

By continuously delivering memorable and distinguishable experiences, Fitch has cultivated a highly profitable customer base that keeps coming back time and time again to find out what's next.

Innovation, as it turns out, plays a huge role in The Unexpected. It's not just about being cool; it's also about being relevant and scalable.

San-Francisco-based Uber is one company that is plying innovation as a tool to transform its industry, and it does so by delivering The Unexpected — in its service offerings, the experience and even its very unique business model.

A private livery service founded in 2009 on the premise that there was a better way for seamless travel within a city, Uber's take on transportation combined with a keen understanding of how to weave storytelling into social media has helped the company expand from one city to 250 worldwide in a very brief period of time.

The premise is simple: Download the Uber app onto your smartphone. When you need a ride, power up the app and click a button. You don't even need to know where you are because the app interfaces with your smartphone's GPS and connects you with a nearby driver who can offer a ride in their car. The service offers everything from basic upscale car models to taxis, SUVs and even luxury cars, depending on the city.

The app allows you to track the driver's location on your phone and watch them approach. Or, you can forgo the phone watching and wait for a text message from Uber that informs you that your ride has arrived.

Once you've reached your destination, use the app to pay your fare. No tip is necessary, and no cash or credit card changes hands. If you're travelling with a friend or colleague, you can even split the fare — at the touch of a button.

Part of Uber's brilliance is its management team's recognition that soliciting instant feedback keeps the experience top-of-mind, and that using social media built into the app makes that feedback viral.

Add to that a strong hyper-local community — Uber segments its website into city-focused portals, each with its own blog and each connected to local social media channels where feedback is streamed to share users' experiences.

A deeper dive reveals that Uber's business model is just as innovative. The company owns no vehicles and employs no full-time drivers. It's basically a networked, GPS-driven booking service that takes a commission for facilitating the transaction, so it's no wonder that today Uber is valued at nearly $40 billion.

Every step along the way, Uber delivers The Unexpected for travelers. In July 2013, for example, Uber's New York City market partnered with a helicopter company to offer an Uberchopper service. Starting on the Fourth of July weekend, users could tap a button and request a private driver to transport them and four friends to a helipad, where the Uberchopper took off for the Hamptons. Another driver, awaiting their arrival, took them to their next destination. The company continued its service offerings in the Hamptons, saying, "What better way to get from the beach to the bar than your own private driver, requested on-demand."

At just over $3,000 per person, the surprise offering was a smash hit, and Uber eventually extended the Uberchopper service through the end of the summer.

When you look at the top employers across America, many of them are highly ranked not because they're the nation's highest wage payers, rather, it's the other things they do — the non-traditional benefits they offer, the ways they train, plus other intangibles, like the ways they empower staff members, the philosophies they use to develop and unleash innovation — to deliver new experiences to customers that makes them so special.

The closer you look, the more you recognize how their commitment to internal and external service — specifically delivering The Unexpected by building cultures where The Unexpected thrives — defines them.

At Rochester, New York-based Wegmans, which operates more than 80 grocery stores in six states, employee empowerment is built into the fabric of this family-owned business' corporate culture. Team members are encouraged to identify and act upon opportunities to deliver memorable experiences to both customers and suppliers. They even have the latitude to reward one another with gift cards when they see above-and-beyond service delivery taking place.

As a result, turnover at Wegmans is less than 3.5 percent. Employees consider the company their extended family. And Wegmans consistently ranks near the top of *Fortune*'s annual Best Companies to Work For list. What's most impressive is that the company does all this in one of the toughest industries with one of the slimmest profit margins.

This surprise-and-delight-the-customer attitude flourishes at Sunnyvale, California-based NetApp, one of the most creative technology companies in the world.

In 2008, NetApp created the vice chairman position for its then company president, Silicon Valley icon Tom Mendoza. The idea was that Mendoza would focus solely on customer advocacy initiatives, partner with NetApp sales and channel partners to deliver more value to customers, and champion the company's values and leadership to employees.

In the five years since his position's establishment, Mendoza has cemented NetApp's reputation as an employer-of-choice in the valley. He cultivated a culture that empowered NetApp's front-line team members to deliver The Unexpected whenever possible.

And to keep it top-of-mind, Mendoza asks company managers to let him know when they notice an employee creating memorable moments for a customer, vendor or even a fellow employee. Mendoza calls those employees and thanks them for their initiative and effort — sometimes making as many calls as 20 per day.

Consider what's happening at Portland, Oregon's Umpqua Bank, which counts its daily "motivation moment" as central to its efforts to distinguish itself from the competition by fostering a workplace where employees think and act differently than those at other banks.

Every morning, team members gather and share their stories of exceptional customer service delivery. They recognize each other's achievements, set common goals and spend a few minutes together having fun. The ritual builds a tight-knit community, rewards innovation and creativity, and builds upon the bank's growing collection of legendary service stories. The result is a motivated workforce that has helped Umpqua deliver consistent growth, and a key reason why in September 2013 it was well-positioned to acquire Sterling Financial Corp. and create the West Coast's largest community bank.

Just 7 percent of consumers say that customer service experiences they have with companies typically exceed their expectations.
Source: Echo/ American Express Global Customer Service Barometer

And then there is the Methodist Hospital System in Houston, Texas. A few years ago, CEO Dr. Marc Boom wrote his own magical moment when the newly named chief executive distributed debit cards preloaded with $200 to every employee as a way of recognizing the staff's efforts to promote the health system's I Care philosophy.

Unexpected gestures like this helped secure a place for Methodist Hospital System on *Fortune*'s list.

The bottom line is that winners don't become winners by accident. They are methodical, strategic and deliberate in their actions.

Most important, success is not dependent on your ability to deliver The Unexpected every moment of every day. It all comes down to empowering front-line employees and developing internal systems that allow you and your team to find ways to deliver it. Execution requires finding opportunities and then making the most of them. When you do this, your company will establish its essential differentiator in the marketplace and be well on its way to leaving the competition in the dust.

2 Because It Makes Me Feel Good

Human beings are creatures of emotion rather than thought. Sure, most of the time our rational mind controls our irrational mind or else we'd be little more than highly capable beasts. But, for the most part, our actions are dictated by how we feel more often than by what we think. It is, in essence, that age-old struggle of Dr. Jekyll and Mr. Hyde. Who will have the upper hand? Truth be told, no one is all Jekyll or all Hyde, nature demands a balance of some degree.

At a basic level, our brains are hard-wired to be led by our feelings. Things that are pleasing, we want more of; things that are not or that cause pain, we avoid. Building the mental- or self-discipline to recognize and overcome that is difficult, even for the most fine-tuned, stoic executive. It's no wonder why some business leaders get branded as hot heads while others earn reputations as having the ability to stay cool under pressure. And it is here where our overwhelmingly positive reaction to The Unexpected lives and breathes.

Consider The Ritz-Carlton Hotel Co. "The Ritz-Carlton charges $500 a night for rooms," says Randi Busse, founder and president of Workforce Development Group Inc., a Long Island, New York-based customer service and client retention organization. Workforce Development Group works with small- to mid-sized companies, associations and chambers of commerce to enhance customer experiences and to increase client retention rates by focusing on service as a differentiator.

"The Ritz-Carlton charges $500 a night for rooms. And right next door to The Ritz-Carlton may be a Holiday Inn that's charging $159 a night," says Busse. "People will drive past the Holiday Inn to stay in The Ritz-Carlton because they have this feeling that it will be a better experience.

"Maybe there are nicer beds in The Ritz-Carlton. And maybe I'm getting chocolates on my pillow. But the reality is that people do not shop price unless that's all they shop. They shop experience," Busse explains. "Studies show that people are willing to pay more — without batting an eyelash — for that really great experience. And when you ask people why they stay at The Ritz-Carlton over the Holiday Inn, all things being equal, they'll tell you, 'Because it makes me feel good.'"

> The Unexpected is the unanticipated reward that grabs attention and initiates a bond

So why is this instinctual need to feel good so important? And how does it relate to delivering The Unexpected?

A lot of research over the years has focused on the effect The Unexpected has on a person's neurology. One of the most well-known studies was conducted by F. Gregory Ashby, Vivian V. Valentin and And U. Turken of the University of California at Santa Barbara and Stanford University.

The trio proposed a neuropsychological theory that an unexpected, non-contingent reward, such as receiving an unanticipated gift, causes dopamine to be released from brain stem sites, which results in an elevation in positive mood — essentially creating joy and happiness.

Business and industry today have taken note of these findings and started to recognize just how powerful delivering The Unexpected can be for their respective organizations.

"What's interesting to me about how neuroscience is evolving into business and workplace applications is that this hard core science of understanding how the brain works is now able to be applied to neuro-marketing, which is the science of understanding why people make the purchasing decisions that they do," says Alicia Arenas, founder and CEO of Sanera, The People Development Co. It is the driving force behind developing products and services around user experience.

Based in San Antonio, Arenas has applied her human resources experience at *Fortune* 100 and *Fortune* 500 companies toward mentoring, coaching and strategizing with executives at organizations of all sizes to help them maximize how their people deliver service to customers. In 2010, Arenas was selected as one of five bloggers from around the nation to audit the Disney Institute's curriculum and provide feedback to program executives on how they deliver service to the consumer.

"It's fascinating, really," she says. "The science has led to an answer, which is emotions. It is all about emotions. People don't make the purchasing decisions that they make because they've done a double-blind taste test. They do it because of how a product or a service makes them feel. This has shown us that it's what we really need to be doing to be different, and what we really need to tap into to wow the consumer."

That's because when you're doing something unexpected, it creates in the other person an element of surprise and joy. And when that happens, your brand becomes cemented in the consumer's mind as a brand that is joyfully surprising.

"It's amazing that we're now able to understand that these emotional imprints in the brain are what compel people to have brand loyalty," Arenas says. "If you're able to capture someone's surprise, and you're able to instill joy in what they're doing, it cements itself in the brain, in the limbic system, and that translates into a subconscious desire in the individual to continue to do things with that brand."

Companies like Starbucks have understood this relationship for years and woven delivery of The Unexpected into the very fabric of its culture.

"I'm a frequent Starbucks person," says Mary Jo Bitner, Ph.D., of the University of Arizona. "I stopped in the other day and noticed that they had the new Howard Schultz book ["Onward: How Starbucks Fought for Its Life without Losing Its Soul"] available there. I have his other book, so I was thinking I wanted to get that book at some point. I was going to order it on Amazon, but I saw it right there in the store while I was getting coffee and just grabbed it, asked for my coffee and the barista said, 'Pick out a gift card.'"

Bitner, who is the Edward M. Carson Chair in Service Marketing at Arizona State University W.P. Carey School of Business and co-founder and executive director of the university's Center for Services Leadership, was frankly a bit taken aback at first.

"I said, 'I didn't ask for a gift card. I don't want a gift card.'"

But the barista just shook his head.

"No, ma'am," he said. "You get a $5 gift card just for buying the book here in the store.

"That was something completely unexpected," she says.

Surprising Bitner, widely considered one of the world's foremost authorities on world-class customer service, isn't easy. As co-author of "Services Marketing: Integrating Customer Focus Across the Firm" (McGraw-Hill, Fourth Edition, 2006), a leading text in services marketing used at universities across the U.S. and worldwide, Bitner is acknowledged as one of the founders and leaders in the study of services marketing.

"They weren't advertising a free gift card with every book purchase, at least as far as I could tell," she says. "It was so out of the ordinary from what I was expecting, yet, Starbucks has built a reputation on doing those little things that surprise customers and, well, just makes them smile. I know I did."

Another way Starbucks delivers The Unexpected is by rewarding its loyal customers — those who use the Starbucks pre-loaded charge card. The company regularly sends out gift certificate postcards to its members who make stopping in for must-have lattes and mochas part of their daily or weekly routine.

Instead of turning their experience into something predictable — for example, a free cup of coffee certificate every time $100 is spent — Starbucks takes a different tack. Its promotions include free specialty beverages, samples of new offerings and discounts on seasonal items. Better yet, the company seemingly sends out these postcard gift certificates at random, not necessarily tying them to members spending a specific dollar amount within a certain period of time or reaching a definitive goal.

The net result is that when you ask loyal Starbucks' consumers why their neighborhood store is the place of choice, they point to two main things — the experience they have with each encounter and, just as important, how interacting with Starbucks makes them feel. Not surprisingly, few people mention the coffee.

Video game designers and online retailers also catered to this phenomenon years ago, long before it became fashionable, according to Kes Sampanthar, director of media strategy for Cynergy Systems.

Sampanthar's Washington, D.C.-based firm develops what it calls "rich Internet applications" that use trademarked approaches to the concept, design and development processes of software. Called ThinkFirst and LookFirst, both are intended to enhance an end user's experience and deliver The Unexpected. Cynergy counts among its clientele companies such as SAP, eBay, Microsoft, Adobe and IBM, all well-known for delivering world-class customer service — and often The Unexpected — to clients.

"We started looking into what we call motivational design," explains Sampanthar. "And the research was how unexpected service or unexpected rewards fire up the brain."

Sampanthar looked at video game designers, which for years built into the games reward schedules and unexpected rewards to systematically surprise game players and cause them to become further engaged, wondering what they could possibly find next.

"Nobody had really put this all together to understand how these systems actually work," Sampanthar says. "Nobody had figured out what exactly is the unexpected reward and why it is that important."

His research unearthed something fascinating: An unexpected reward fires a dopamine circuit and tells the brain to pay attention.

"It says that this is something important and potentially a new source of excitement," Sampanthar says. "So (the brain) pays attention to everything that happened right before that reward happened and tries to repeat it."

But then, because that reward was designed to be unexpected, there is no repeat of it.

"And when that unexpected reward doesn't happen, the brain begins to look for other ways to create that trigger," he says. "It's almost like an important Post-It note gets put in the brain that says, 'This is important. Pay attention.'"

This is exactly what happened when Apple Inc. introduced the first iPod.

"It was sowing this experience [in people], which was so far removed from anything else people had experienced," Sampanthar says. "Never mind every other MP3 player that had preceded it. This (the iPod) was a new experience for how we listened to music, and it was so unexpected from what had come before. Suddenly, here was something that really fired our brains to pay attention to why was this so far removed from what we'd always expected before its launch."

The same goes for retail stores like Seattle-based Nordstrom.

"When we go to a place like Nordstrom, we're actually expecting something different, though we don't know what," Sampanthar says. "Nordstrom goes out of its way to tell its staff to do things outside the norm."

An often-told Nordstrom story involves a person who returned a set of tires to Nordstrom despite the fact that Nordstrom doesn't sell tires. It is a story that has gone viral and has been etched in the minds of everyone who has heard it. It might have cost them several hundred dollars, but the publicity they received because of it is likely valued in the millions. Beyond this, they also have done such things as wrap presents — at no charge — for items that weren't even purchased at its store. It's the empowerment of Nordstrom's front-line employees to identify and act upon opportunities that has led to this.

"When we walk in somewhere," Sampanthar says, "our brains are constantly making these predictions of what it's going to experience. And the general experience in most business scenarios, or customer or consulting scenarios, is that we're constantly making these predictions of what's going to happen.

"If we walk into a shop and somebody does something unexpected, our brain pays a lot of attention to that." And, something else that Sampanthar learned from his research: "We treat that company that delivers The Unexpected the same way we'd treat a person who just did something amazing, kind or thoughtful towards us.

"We attribute that to the company," he says. "Our brain makes a note to remember that, moving forward, I'm also going to give the warm, emotional feeling I had towards the unexpected reward towards the company."

70% of buying experiences are based on how the customer feels they are being treated.
Source: McKinsey & Co.)

Our brains are funny things. They can be fooled. They can be manipulated. But they react predictably to positive experiences, which business leaders must pay attention to if they want to differentiate themselves from the competition.

"It's that warm, fuzzy feeling, like any gift that's truly an unexpected gift when it shows up," adds Stephen Antisdel, a partner at Precept Partners, a Michigan-based consulting firm comprised of serial entrepreneurs who have built numerous Internet businesses and e-commerce sites.

"It is so unlike a traditional anniversary present in that if you have it on the exact day you expect you're going to get a gift, it's nice, but it doesn't really get your blood flowing. How much more exciting is it when it is months removed from one of these days a gift from someone just shows up? It stirs the heart. You have a deep feeling of appreciation. It really is a different psychology when it's truly unexpected."

But, Antisdel warns, "That's the challenge for any of us as business people — figuring out how to deliver it."

3 Delivering The Unexpected

Making promises is easy — just ask Bernie Madoff — but delivering on promises is where things get tricky. As entrepreneurs, we make promises every day — to vendors, employees, partners, prospects and customers. And we are expected to deliver upon those promises — excuse-free.

So to reach these goals we build systems that are designed to create superior customer service in our organizations. We have systems that ensure vendors are paid on time by our accounts payable departments. We use systems to make employee payroll and human resource benefits delivery seamless and reliable. And we rely on systems so that our companies' operations deliver promised products and services on time and on budget so that our prospects and customers keep coming back.

Efficient systems, however, are not enough.

A corporate culture that embraces The Unexpected is just as important. And in order to truly differentiate oneself from the competition and build loyal customers for life, an organization's corporate culture must be built upon a foundation where delivering world-class customer service is the cornerstone.

When this happens, delivering consistent, world-class customer service becomes the norm. But world-class customer service today is only the price of entry. After you've anted the entrance fee, to increase profitability and market share you must occasionally surprise your customers, vendors and employees. The best way to do this is by providing them with something that they're not expecting — when they expect it least.

All of this probably sounds wonderful, but before you can build and implement these systems or create a culture where The Unexpected is ingrained in its fabric, there is a bigger question that must be answered: What exactly comprises The Unexpected?

Sure, it makes you feel good. And yes, you know it when you see it or experience it. But neither of those factors will help you build a competent system that effectively allows you to deliver The Unexpected. To do this, you must first understand what goes into making it real.

Four key components make up The Unexpected. Properly delivered it becomes:

- Memorable.
- Distinguishable.
- Viral.
- Profitable.

A really different and emotionally meaningful service wows the customer.

Memorable

People remember something that is experiential. The extraordinary experience, itself, is ingrained in their memories, becoming inclusionary parts of the stories they relate to others. In essence, this is the "what" of The Unexpected. With my JetBlue experience, this is when my team members heard the captain's voice over the public announcement system saying pizzas were en route to the plane. The unbelievable nature of that moment caught them off guard, etching itself into their memories and taking on a life of its own. Think of it as the moment when the legend was created.

In their ground-breaking 1998 work, *The Experience Economy*, B. Joseph Pine and James H. Gilmore theorized that a new economy lay on the horizon — one with a focus on businesses orchestrating memorable events for their customers.

Because services were quickly becoming commoditized, Pine and Gilmore said that the memory, itself, becomes the product being peddled — the "experience."

So, by the time the pizzas arrived, the actual act of eating a slice or two acted as the final element to seal the experience that began when the pilot announced the pizza delivery, continued with the visual experience of seeing the trucks drive up the tarmac to the plane, and then became real as the flight attendants served slices to each passenger.

Distinguishable

Because The Unexpected is memorable, people remember the organization — or person — who delivers it as uniquely qualified to do so. This serves to boost a brand and acts as a differentiator when it comes to comparing two companies that provide similar services within the same market space.

Think about Starbucks. When you compare it against another coffee store, such as Dunkin' Donuts, you have a mental image of what each brand represents. Despite any preconceived notions, Dunkin' Donuts serves coffee that many claim to be just as delicious as Starbucks. But in the mainstream, Dunkin' Donuts' brand fails to have the same level of brand cachet attached to Starbucks. When you think about service and experience in the coffee industry, the first name that pops into nearly every consumer's head is Starbucks.

And then there is Nordstrom. Strip its name from the store marquee and just compare its merchandise to any other high-end department store in the world. What you'll find is that the clothing and accessories carried often are at the same or higher quality than Nordstrom. Yet, say "Nordstrom" and what you think about is the service legend that's been created.

By delivering The Unexpected, companies such as Starbucks or Nordstrom forge a very valuable brand that can be leveraged as a powerful — and profitable — differentiator.

Viral

Everybody loves a story. The Unexpected offers a great opportunity to tell one.

Not long ago, when you had an experience — good or bad — you would share it with others on a one-to-one or one-to-many basis, depending on your physical location. This could be at a social function or family affair, and it could be days, weeks or months after the experience. The more incredible the experience, the more ingrained the story becomes in your own mind. If the airline lost your luggage, the waitress spilled coffee in your lap or the clerk refused to accept your returned item, over drinks or dinner, you would recount your story and the listeners would shake their heads and commiserate. Maybe, they would even tell you about terrible service experiences they might have received themselves.

After the recounting, people may or may not remember the stories, and those that do may or may not choose to give their business to the specific organizations mentioned. The time element — passing the story along well after the event took place — combined with the one-to-one of limited audience nature of spreading the information, diluted the overall impact of the message.

But now fast-forward to today. We live in a faster-paced, uber-connected world where technology has changed the rules. When the same experience happens now, people spread the word in an instant. In fact, they might still be in the middle of experiencing that negative service when they begin to tweet it out to their followers, updating their Facebook status or letting their LinkedIn business contacts know what is happening. Now, what happened in the present is communicated rather than what happened in the past.

Clearly, some experiences are stickier than others, but when The Unexpected occurs, the reality is that people can't wait to tell somebody what happened to them as quickly as possible. There's a magical energy to storytelling that has been part of our being since the earliest days of mankind. And because of both the power of The Unexpected and the ability to convey the story in near real time, this rise of social media and social networking has become a true game-changer when it comes to the viral nature of sharing the experience of The Unexpected.

Profitable

As we move toward an economy where standard — or even world-class — customer service is your price of entry, only those companies that deliver The Unexpected will be able to command premium pricing for their goods and services and gain market share.

Gilmore and Pine argue that this is the next evolution for those businesses that learn how to effectively deliver the "experience." More advanced experience-oriented businesses, they say, can begin charging for the value of the transformation that the experience offers. In the case of a Starbucks or Nordstrom, when was the last time you actually thought about the price you were paying to do business with them? You simply turned over your $4 or $5, picked up your venti skinny vanilla latte, and went on your merry way.

Customer service expert and author John DiJulius puts it this way in his book, *What's the Secret?: To Providing a World-Class Customer Experience*: "When you compete on price, you attract customers who are opportunistic and looking for the best deal. Margins are too thin today to compete on price. On the other hand, if you choose to compete on experience, you eliminate over 80 percent of your competition, who are cutting costs and service trying to be the cheapest."

Therefore, according to DiJulius, you can keep your prices at a premium, your margins strong, and your company profitable when you deliver The Unexpected. More important, you do not commoditize your organization's products or services.

4 Why the Time is NOW for The Unexpected

There is a sad truth about customer service that has crept into nearly every corner of today's society — we settle for just OK rather than seeking out the truly exceptional.

Why are we surprised when the clerk at the drug store looks us in the eye? Why are we happy when we receive service that, at best, ranks slightly above average? And why are we shocked when a live person answers the phone during a call to customer service?

"Consumers are incredibly underwhelmed with what they receive," says Michael Brunner, CEO of Pittsburgh-based Brunner Inc., an independent, full-service advertising agency that represents such organizations as Zippo, Bob Evans, Huffy and GNC.

"What's happened is that technology created the belief that customer service would be more advanced, better suited, more customized, more specific and more in sync with the individual," Brunner says. "But that's just not the case."

Instead, Brunner suggests we look at customer service trends like this: Draw a curved line upward with an arrow at the end. This represents technology. The dramatic surge upward represents the speed at which technology is advancing — quickly. Consumers were led to believe that with this technological advance the level of service would improve along a parallel line.

However, that's not what happened.

Above the technology arrow, draw another curved arrow, this one arcing downward. This arrow represents the quality of service being delivered.

"There has been a tremendous disappointment and feeling of a lack of customization and personalization through customer service despite the advancements in technology," Brunner says. "We're seeing this every day. We are reaching the point where there is an expanding gap — the more technology advances, the greater the disappointment there is with the consumer as to what their expectation is and what they receive as it relates to their own experiences."

This, Brunner further explains, can be anything from the phone call to their bank, utility company, cable provider or local government entity. "The overall experience has most likely declined as improvements to the technology used to deliver products and services have increased. This is a bad trend."

This is why the time is now to deliver The Unexpected.

And in business, timing is everything.

As proof, think back just a decade or so ago to the hey-day of the dot-com era. Just like the Roaring '20s, the good times were never going to end. All it took to raise a quick million or two was the nut of an idea scribbled out on the back of a napkin or envelope. Financial projections didn't even have to be real — they just needed to sound real. Investors begged stockbrokers to find ways to get them in on the latest tech initial public offering — hoping to cash out with a double-or triple-digit increase by the end of a single day. Fortunes were made — and lost — in hours. But all of that came to an end in March 2000, when the bubble finally burst. Within two years, the Great Shakeout finally separated the pretenders from the performers.

Looking back, it's easy to see how unrealistic the financial business models of well-known busts (pets.com, InfoSpace, theGlobe.com, Freeinternet.com, Boo.com and Webvan, etc.) really were. And though it required a massive bubble burst to create the needed worldwide reality check, there were some bright spots. From a timing perspective, the period from 1998 to 2000, with low interest rates and available capital, provided an opportunity for swift development of the backbone that powers today's digital world.

And there were companies that came to prominence during the mid-to-late '90s; Google, Amazon.com and eBay emerged and became corporate powerhouses that continue to innovate today. Apple piggybacked on the digital music revolution to capture prominence in the personal music experience market (overtaking Sony Walkman's/Discman's former dominance) with the iPod, leading the way for a litany of innovations. And, the seeds were sown for what would ultimately become Facebook and LinkedIn.

Spontaneous and generous gestures produce puppy-dog appreciative customers.

Today, while we're not standing precariously on any new Internet bubble, we are once again at a rare moment in time — a moment in time uniquely positioned for companies that deliver The Unexpected.

Consider for a moment how social media has become today's great equalizer — especially when it comes to customer service.

"It takes everything, creates a half-life, and accelerates it dramatically," Brunner says. "A negative experience that a customer feels today will be delivered to thousands of people in a singular moment. That can create a swell, bad feeling or bandwagon that others can jump on board with and begin saying the same thing. This channel didn't really exist just five years ago the same way that it does today."

So what if we are able to find a way to take advantage of this moment in time, view it as an opportunity, and turn the notion of spreading bad news around? What if we take positive, unexpected experiences and use social media to differentiate our organization from our competitors? With so much bad customer service out there, it's not hard. An organization with even a modicum of understanding about how social media works can leverage its ability to deliver The Unexpected and build a simple communication program around it.

First, understand how people use social media. When your organization delivers The Unexpected to customers, vendors and employees, there's a very good chance that they will spread the word with others about it. Set up alerts that monitor your company's name, product or service. Then, capture that information in some meaningful way and design a platform to use for your own communications.

> It is 6 to 7 times more costly to attract a new customer than it is to retain an existing one.
> Source: White House Office of Consumer Affairs

Properly used, this can become a rallying point for your employees. Sharing news of The Unexpected with your vendors, investors or clients shows your constituents in other people's words what you want to convey about yourself. It brings The Unexpected out of the shadows and into the light — letting others know about it.

"You can use this to your advantage," Brunner says. "These are opportune times that need to be identified quickly and responded to immediately. They're not going to come around too often."

And, as with anything in business that relies on timing, once the time to strike is past, it's too late to go back and capture the moment again. After all, who wouldn't have liked to have purchased Apple stock for $27 per share in December 2009 instead of the more than $100 per share in 2014? It's even more impressive when you consider that in February 2015 the company became the first to reach $700 billion in market value!

5 How Any Industry Can Deliver The Unexpected

By now you're probably saying to yourself, "How can I deliver The Unexpected? I could certainly use extra market share and customers for life." The good news is, no matter what industry you're in or what type of company you run, The Unexpected is universally adaptable. You can deliver unexpected service at an accounting firm. You can deliver it at a law firm. You can be a rolled steel manufacturer, financial services firm, investment bank, sandwich shop, sandwich shop franchisor or even an online retailer.

Whatever product you sell or service you offer, accomplishing The Unexpected requires three things: First, you must have a servant culture. This is different than the traditional notion of servant leadership, where leadership is a sacrificial position and the leader's primary role becomes to serve his or her team. Rather, in a servant culture, each employee is empowered by their leader to take it upon him or herself to act in the best interest of the customer and consequently make decisions that positively impact every customer's experience with the organization.

Second, along the same lines, you must empower people on the front lines to identify opportunities to make creative and innovative decisions on how to deliver service to clients. Innovation is the difference maker when it comes to The Unexpected because delivering surprise and delight requires doing what hasn't been done before.

Finally, you must formalize systems within your company that allow for these things to occur. This includes having processes in place that ensure consistent delivery of above-average to world-class service and thereby allow every team member to search out and identify unique opportunities to deliver The Unexpected when they are able to take that extra step.

When it comes to execution, it all begins and ends with your people.

As with anything service-related, delivering The Unexpected relies on two things — either hiring the right type of person to work within your organization or understanding how to train your existing employees to identify and act upon opportunities to deliver The Unexpected. No matter how great, reliable or seamless your systems may be, you simply cannot deliver The Unexpected without an organization filled with like-minded individuals who buy into the idea.

"Fundamentally, it's all about making it important and empowering the front-line employees to deliver it," says Chip Bell, founder of The Chip Bell Group and author or co-author of more than 19 books on customer service. "There's enormous creativity at the front line, the kind that delivers The Unexpected when the opportunity arises. But no matter how creative that front-line person might be, unless they've got the authority and resources to do it, it's not likely to happen."

Beyond that, it's also a matter of developing authentic customer-centric relationships.

"You need to develop a system that allows you to know your customers," Bitner says. "And I mean not just know your customers in a superficial way. Instead, know them from a deeper relationship perspective gained by research, conversations and observations."

Bitner says those systems should also include everything from your organization's physical space, design elements, technology and training.

That's exactly the approach Chris Zane, owner of Zane's Cycles, takes.

"Everything boils down to the relationship we have with our employees and our customers," explains Zane, whose Branford, Connecticut-based bike shop is renowned for its focus on building a bond with each and every customer. "When we look at the relationship with an employee, I like to say that there are two kinds of people — the eyes-down people and the eyes-up people."

Eyes-down people are those who look down. "The minute they see something coming into their peripheral vision, they don't want to take responsibility for it," says Zane. "They want to have someone else take care of it because they're doing something else."

Contrast that with the eyes-up person, who is engaged and wants to interact with people.

"He or she is friendly and upbeat, and knows that their responsibility is to take care of the customer," Zane explains.

These are the people Zane hires for his company, which has grown from a local bicycle and hobby shop into the largest Premiums and Incentives bicycle distributor in the country. They are also the type of people who are motivated to identify opportunities — as well as new ways — to deliver The Unexpected in any organization.

Eyes-up people energize organizations. They are always looking for new ways to delight and surprise the customer — not only because it is good for the organization, but also because they truly like doing it. As a result, their energy — and attitude — becomes viral.

When you're working with existing employees, find ways to teach people to become "eyes up" rather than "eyes down." Show them how there is a great thrill involved with delivering The Unexpected. Let them see how it is incredibly satisfying for the person delivering it, as well as the company. You may not be able to convert everyone, but as each existing team member sees the successes and experiences that feeling, the number of people who will want to learn how to do it, too, will expand exponentially.

Next, develop and implement systems that allow you to deliver high-end customer service as a non-negotiable item. If you're not delivering world-class customer service on a consistent basis, the only thing that delivering The Unexpected will accomplish is to draw attention to an organization that is suddenly exposed for its subpar — or at best average — customer service. It is more likely a recipe for disaster than a formula for building customers for life.

Explains Zane: "We train employees about the products that we offer and we train them about the focus of the products and the services we offer. We also train them about how they should approach interacting with the customers. Because they're good people, smart people and friendly people, they get it and become very valuable to our organization."

> Delivering The Unexpected means more than just occasionally wowing clients; it means wowing employees and acknowledging them when they've delivered distinguishable surprise and delight.

Zane views this system that delivers consistent and reliable world-class service as his initial competitive advantage, and a key reason why he's built customers for life.

"That's really the thing that my competitors have a really hard time (with), because they get these great technical guys that (are) 'eyes down' working on a bike, never looking up, and just not creating a relationship," he says. "So the customer feels like they're not in an environment where they're welcome or they're appreciated. They feel like they're in an environment (where) they're taking time away from the mechanic or the person in the store doing their job. And that's really been where our success has come from — from our employees interacting and engaging the customer in a relationship."

But a smart and responsible approach to system building also requires comprehensive training in both service and financial management. Employees must understand what impacts the bottom line, and how.

"You have to give them information about how the business works," explains Paul Shrater, the co-founder and executive vice president of Minimus.biz, an online retailer and wholesaler of more than 2,500 different travel-sized and individual-sized products, such as snacks, groceries and cosmetics. "Empowering a person who doesn't understand how to make good decisions can be terrible. Too often, entrepreneurs and business leaders forget about that piece."

You can accomplish this without breaking the bank by offering basic balance sheet management training, like P&L 101 or an entry-level accounting course. What you'll find is that when employees understand how their actions impact the financial side of your business, it directly translates back to one of the four tenets of The Unexpected — profitability.

In Zane's case, he has even assigned a dollar value to each potential customer.

"Every customer who comes through my door is worth $12,500," he says. "If I get all the bikes from them that they're going to buy from the time they get their first bike until they get their retirement bike, and all the accessories that go along with it, we believe that the number is $12,500."

It's simple, measurable, and is communicated to all employees who work for Zane's Cycles.

"That allows my employees to look at the customer differently because it's not a $6 tube customer or $1.69 power bar customer," Zane says. "That's a $12,500 relationship that we want to continue to have. And so we're going to do whatever we have to do to keep that customer satisfied and happy in our environment so that return continues."

Not every organization can easily connect a value to each customer. It requires time and a serious commitment to aligning an organization's sales, customer service, operations, training systems and management operations. However, that doesn't mean attaining it is out of reach. Just like delivering The Unexpected, getting a system in place is a matter of better understanding your business, then establishing a solid foundation and philosophy upon which you can build.

And this is the approach that Shrater took with Minimus.biz.

"I held a meeting and we had everyone from the people who pack orders to our customer service representatives to our operations team," he says. "I showed them a pie chart that broke down the information about the financial side in easy-to-understand percentage segments."

Shrater's charts detailed the percentages of what went into every order Minimus.biz processed — shipping, packaging materials, errors, product costs and myriad other items.

"It was eye-opening for many of them," he says. "But they really began to understand how much went into even the simplest order and where our profit came from. From that point forward, people began to talk about how they contributed more effectively and efficiently. And then I started to change their mindset about why it was so important to find ways to go above and beyond and identify ways to deliver things such as unexpected customer service."

And, as with anything significant in business, this requires a commitment from the highest level of any organization. Just like Zane and Shrater, management must set clear expectations and reinforce its importance on a regular basis. If you're set on delivering The Unexpected, commit to it, and then follow through.

With a solid foundation in place — investing in a methodical approach to the people question and a willingness to invest in developing an organization that consistently delivers above-average or world-class customer service — building an organization capable of delivering The Unexpected becomes not just possible, but even a little bit easier.

Doing this requires four additional steps:

Teach every employee on your team why The Unexpected is important to the company's growth and profitability, as well its future.

Show your team how to recognize The Unexpected and how to identify opportunities for delivering it.

Empower every employee at every level to deliver The Unexpected when he or she believes it proper to do so.

Reinforce delivery of The Unexpected by acknowledging it, acknowledging the people who deliver it, letting them talk about the joy they receive delivering it, and sharing those success stories across the entire organization.

Even so, you cannot plan exactly what The Unexpected will look like. Rather, through a combination of culture and systems, the conditions are set so that when the time is right, you and your employees know how to bring The Unexpected to life.

Teach every employee...

Keep in mind that great leaders are, in essence, great teachers. Pick up any leadership or management book and you'll read that leaders are at their best when they are helping to create new leaders. So, as a great leader, it is incumbent upon you to teach every employee on your team why The Unexpected is important.

Begin by explaining why delivering The Unexpected separates your company from other companies like this:

- Successful businesses are a small group in the larger business pool today.
- There are fewer customers for the same amount of retail or service space.
- Those who communicate what they do different from the competition have an advantage over those who simply compare themselves as "me, too" organizations.
- The best way to communicate your story so that people want to come to you and price is not the overall driving factor is by being exceptional — and that means delivering The Unexpected.
- Your customer becomes evangelistic and looks for people to bring to your brand.

Show your team...

Next, demonstrate to team members from all levels of the organization how to recognize The Unexpected by providing examples of it in action. Be clear that you do not want your employees to mimic the examples they see.

Instead, explain that by recognizing The Unexpected when it happens, your expectation is that team members will be prepared to take the next logical step — to identify opportunities for delivering it and adapting the examples they've seen to each unique situation.

Just as important, explain that delivering The Unexpected doesn't mean delivering it every second or minute of every day. It is spontaneous, and each situation is unique. Think of it like an improv class — you start and adapt to where it goes.

Here's an example: On a Delta Air Lines flight out of Calgary, my wife, Joan, wanted some tea. The flight attendant told her they had just one flavor available. It wasn't a flavor Joan wanted. But then the stewardess smiled at my wife and said, "Every morning, I take from my home five tea bags because sometimes somebody wants something special. So, would you like green tea, herbal tea or one of the other flavors I brought with me?"

Joan and I were taken by surprise. Sure, the tea bags cost maybe 50 cents each, but who does that? Who brings tea bags from home in case passengers or customers want something different than what your organization offers?

This is why people need to see examples before you send them off into action. They need to understand that the size of The Unexpected really doesn't matter. What matters is that when there is an opportunity to deliver something people aren't expecting that will delight and surprise them, find a way to do it.

It's also worth a reminder that you don't deliver The Unexpected for the immediate gain. But you do need to be cognizant of where your opportunities exist, as well as why specific opportunities may be more important than others.

If you're committed to The Unexpected, you do it primarily because you believe in it. This is an "all-in" initiative, and you can't do it halfway. Delivering The Unexpected means you are committing yourself and your organization to doing something that no one else will do.

"Customer service shouldn't just be a department, it should be the entire company."
—Tony Hsieh, CEO, Zappos

At Zane's Cycles, when someone comes into the store because they need a bolt or a nut or washer for a bicycle project they're working on at home, Zane says, "We happily hand them the parts they're looking for and tell them it's no charge.

"It's only a couple pennies worth of parts or materials for us," Zane says. "They give us an odd look and then smile, appreciating the fact that we're not nickel-and-diming our customers. We've realized that this type of small investment creates a memorable experience for them. They remember we took the time to show them that we care by doing something they didn't expect." Just like at Zane's Cycles, you will soon realize that people who come in don't always need to be charged for the little things.

When you're working with your team, it is also important to keep in mind that some people by nature are more opportunistic than others. This doesn't mean that you can't teach everyone in your organization to deliver The Unexpected. But you should be cognizant that some people will be better able to both identify and deliver it.

One surefire way to spur along others who are not as innately gifted is to personally deliver to them something unexpected. Leave concert tickets, a restaurant gift card or a handwritten note on their desk. Find something small but meaningful that will demonstrate what it means to be the recipient of The Unexpected, as well as how it feels.

People aren't always observant. Sometimes you need to help them pay attention to other areas while they do their job. Sometimes it's not obvious to them what makes somebody surprised. But when you teach employees how to be more observant, you will find that they begin to see things through a completely new lens.

Empower every employee...

When your organization is equipped with a new set of open eyes, it's time to unleash everyone's potential. This is a critical component to achieving success, and therefore no small feat.

Empowering employees at every level of an organization can be challenging — and often scary — for entrepreneurs. That's because it means placing nearly unfettered decision-making power — with potentially significant financial implications — in the hands of every member of an organization. But it is also having them understand that, just like Nordstrom, this is an investment opportunity that your company can make. If it's done without restraint, it can result in a return on investment several hundred-fold.

Not everyone who runs, owns or leads an organization is comfortable with this step, but consider this: In the case of our Delta flight, it wasn't Delta's CEO or top management who provided us with the tea bag solution. Instead, it was a single employee who was empowered to think differently and to be solution-oriented.

It was her observation, combined with an ability to deliver a viable solution on the spot that created the reason why my wife experienced The Unexpected, as well as the reason we continue to share the story with others.

But also be cognizant that part of empowerment is allowing your employees to train themselves.

"We found that when one of our star people really gets it, it's better to let them train the other people in their groups," Shrater says. "Sometimes the manager of that department simply may not be the best person to train those on the front line how to identify opportunities to deliver The Unexpected. When you've got somebody who's actually doing it, why not let them share what they've learned with the others they work with."

Keep in mind, however, when you do empower employees, you must then hold them accountable.

Reinforce delivery...

Finally, it is imperative to acknowledge those who deliver The Unexpected within your organization — both internally to colleagues and externally to customers and vendors. People will see your commitment and belief when they witness regular recognition from your management team.

That human resource side is really a critical piece, Bitner says. "And it must be consistent. You can't reward or incentivize your team one time to deliver something like this," she says. "It has to be built into your system in order for it to be effective."

This can be just about anything — public recognition in some format, something tangible or something monetary. Perhaps it is the creation of an Unexpected Leader of the Month. What matters is that the acknowledgement is significant enough that everybody in the organization is aware that the company as a whole cherishes The Unexpected.

Your management team, including you, must be the group that establishes and follows through with this recognition and acknowledgement component. This demonstrates your belief that delivering The Unexpected is an important part of the organization's culture and a key driver of its success.

This also ties in with the profitability tenet of The Unexpected because acknowledgement leads to loyalty. And loyalty means you have people in your organization who are better trained and will do whatever it takes to get the job done. This combination has a direct correlation to your company being more profitable.

One word of warning: If you don't follow through with the acknowledgement component, then unfortunately it will be all about what you pay your people. A culture of gratitude is an intangible that has tangible positive consequences. Delivering The Unexpected enlivens and energizes that culture. Employees who work in an organization like this say: "It's unbelievable what you do for me."

Whatever method you choose, acknowledge The Unexpected and acknowledge your employees when they make it happen. Make it a continuous activity rather than a one-time event. What you'll find when you do so is that the loyalty this creates becomes part of what makes your company special and differentiates it from the competition.

6 Developing Consistency & Reliability

As I've mentioned in earlier chapters, there is a significant difference between what most would consider world-class customer service and The Unexpected. However, the two are inextricably linked: You must be able to deliver world-class customer service consistently and reliably before you can truly rise to the occasion and deliver The Unexpected.

Consistency, at its most basic level, is the ability to maintain a particular standard or repeat a particular task with minimal variation. Reliability goes hand-in-hand. It is the ability to be trusted to do what is expected or has been promised. Combined, you have a well-regarded organization that delivers customer service at a high level by always doing what it says it is going to do. People must know they can expect quality service and dependable follow through from an organization.

Similarly, consumers see all locations of an organization as a single brand and do not differentiate among locations. They expect the same experience from a Starbucks in Shanghai that they receive from one in Detroit.

This is the new price of entry.

"It sounds pretty simple," says Bitner, "but it's really hard to do. The key to consistently meeting or exceeding expectations is knowing what the expectations are and following those expectations over time. They tend to change.

"Experience is becoming more and more something that people are thinking about. For them, it's not a one-time thing; it's not one event. Rather, it's the total experience based on interaction with different people within an organization, the space, the process and all those other elements that combine to create it. And making sure that is consistent and reliable ... well, that's clearly a challenge unto itself."

For example, let's say you check into a hotel and they give you an upgrade. The room is nice and clean. The maid service is great. And every member of the hotel staff does everything you expect them to do. When you leave, you will remember you received an upgrade and be pleased about it. You might tell someone about it because it's a "nice" story, but there is nothing truly surprising about it as upgrades occur regularly for frequent travelers who stay at luxury hotels. This is, then, world-class customer service, but not The Unexpected.

The same goes with airlines. Let's say the flight is on time. The airline staff members at the airport are polite. They put you in the premier President's Club before you board the plane. And you're upgraded to first class because you're a frequent flyer. It's a great experience, and certainly the moves make your travel easier. But again, this is world-class service, not The Unexpected.

It requires much more than easy upgrades, politeness and traditional above-and-beyond actions to reach the lofty plateau of The Unexpected.

Bitner points to Starbucks, Southwest Airlines, Marriott, Amazon and IKEA as the companies that understand this well.

"The thing that distinguishes them is that they not only deliver customer service consistently, they also consistently look at new ways to innovate around service or to make it fresh so that it's not an old expectation people have when they interact with them," she says. "Instead, it's new and different. Before it can be considered 'unexpected,' it must be innovative."

And, Bitner offers this warning: "If you're just trying to deliver The Unexpected before you've reached that point of consistency, it comes with risk. And that risk is that people will come to expect it. So you need to get used to having expectations raised over and over when it comes to being consistent and reliable — and be able to meet those expectations."

Hortensia Albertini was the founder and chairman of Detroit-based Global LT, a translation and relocation company. She passed away in 2013, but was a true innovator when it came to delivering The Unexpected. Albertini prided herself on her organization's ability to deliver world-class service to clients. Her consistency and reliability helped her attract and retain an impressive roster of clients that represents a full range of global and regional organizations — from small to mid-sized businesses up to the *Fortune* 100.

"You get to know them and you get to anticipate their needs," she explained. "And I think that many times that surprises them — but again, you also have to look for ways to go the extra mile."

That is Global LT's differentiator — going that extra mile and shifting from simply delivering world-class customer service to delivering The Unexpected.

Several years ago, Albertini and her organization were hired to handle the relocation of Dieter Zetsche, Ph.D., the chairman of Daimler AG, from Germany to Michigan. At the time, Zetsche was gaining worldwide appeal from his appearances in television commercials, including the now-famous "Ask Dr. Z" campaign.

Beyond handling the relocation of Zetsche's family, which encompassed full integration, helping to set up housing, enrollment of his children in school, moving all the family's possessions and getting them acclimated to life in Michigan, Albertini went one step further.

"We relocated his daughter's horse as well," she said. "And it wasn't something Zetsche was expecting."

Albertini went to the Hunt Club in Troy, Michigan, herself, to make the necessary arrangements. She told them there was a very important horse coming in. "I wanted to see where the horse was going to be," she said. "I wanted to see the services they offered and make sure they were at the highest possible level. And I wanted to be able to personally tell the family what we had done."

Years later, Zetsche's family still remembers the story and says, "We can't believe (they) transferred our horse." Albertini said. "They were very grateful for what we did."

So the true difference between world-class service and The Unexpected is exactly what you think it would be — everybody expects you to handle all details of an executive and their family's relocation, but nobody expects you to deliver the horse.

> "Customer service is a day in, day out, ongoing, never ending, unremitting, persevering, compassionate, type of activity."
> —Leon Gorman, former CEO, L.L. Bean

When you step back and think about it, Albertini did something that's at the root of delivering The Unexpected: She listened and cared; then went further in order to create a positive and memorable experience.

To be good at this, you need to learn how to be creative. You must think outside the norms of everyday life. And the more often you do it, the better you'll get. But more important, to do this well and consistently you have to care about your customers. Then it becomes easier. And your customers will love it.

In retrospect, it probably cost upwards of $10,000 to bring the horse. But what Albertini received in terms of recognition and client loyalty most likely was worth 10 times that. So you really can't buy the type of recognition delivering The Unexpected brings.

"A lot of people have an insurance agent that sends them a birthday card on their birthday," Bell says. "They obviously know when your birthday is, so that's a good thing. And then there are those agents who call you on your birthday since they know your phone number, too. But one time, my insurance agent had his little girl call me — and she actually sang me happy birthday. That's The Unexpected."

Understanding this concept is one thing; but it's another all together to put it into action. Doing so requires a significant mind shift from the top of an organization to the bottom, and everywhere in between.

"Business leaders at all levels need to start getting comfortable with change," suggests Arenas. "Because the thing about doing The Unexpected is that you can't keep doing it the same way.

"Otherwise, it's not unexpected anymore. When you do the same thing — no matter how impressive — it eventually becomes no longer innovative or creative."

Arenas warns this is a common pitfall for companies and executives who find success delivering The Unexpected — they identify something that works, but then they continue to provide the same thing over and over and don't take the time to innovate or try something new.

"At our core, we are change-resistant creatures," she says. "Leaders who are stuck in tradition and stuck doing things the same way that they have always done them — even if at one time those things were considered unexpected — are not going to propel their companies forward."

So for a hotel or airline to take the leap from world-class service to delivering The Unexpected, it's imperative that their people look for the opportunity to deliver it — and then think about how they can deliver something different each time.

This is one reason why The Ritz-Carlton empowers its employees with up to $2,000 to use as they see fit. Management doesn't equate the actions taken to a specific dollar amount or return on investment. Rather, they recognize the difference between exceptional service and something more.

More important, The Ritz-Carlton understands how its ability to deliver consistent and reliable service puts it in a unique position for staff members to be able to go that extra step and deliver something memorable, distinguishable, viral and profitable. And when you build that upon a solid foundation of being able to deliver consistent and reliable service — and are willing to mix in a bit of innovation and creativity — you have the right foundation to take the next step.

7 Creating the Memorable

It was one of those absolutely gorgeous, hot summer days that look and feel as they were reproduced directly from a Claude Monet masterpiece. I gazed around the offices at our Manchester, New Hampshire co-headquarters and saw our team members plugging away. It was business as usual.

At that moment, I decided to do something special. I called everybody in the office together.

"I heard the blacktop outside is melting," I announced. "You need to get your cars out of the lot now. Do not return."

Immediately, people understood the meaning of my message. A cavalcade of claps, roars and cheers erupted. You could feel the elation spread as a wave across the office. Within minutes, most of our team had gathered up their belongings and headed out to enjoy the day. Others finished up their work and soon followed their colleagues out the door.

Today, people still talk about that moment.

So what makes something that memorable?

At its most basic level, memorable experiences are those that occur outside of the normal interactions you have with an organization. There often is an innovative component because you haven't seen or experienced anything quite like it before. You're surprised and delighted. You want to talk about it with others. And that combination of factors etches the experience in your memory.

My surprise announcement to have team members leave the office and go enjoy the day delivered this type of experience and memory for our staff. It helped build an emotional attachment to CCA Global Partners because it demonstrated through actions — not words — what I thought about them. They were more than simply salaried employees, and I cared about them. This approach has helped CCA Global Partners become an employer-of-choice and led to it being named one of the top companies to work for on three separate occasions.

Let's break it down even further.

First, every employee at any organization expects to receive a paycheck for his or her work. Next, every full-time employee expects to receive some level of benefits, be it health insurance, paid time off or some other common employer-sponsored program. But it's when you do something different for your employees, like offer pet insurance, that the paradigm begins to change.

When you do something that they absolutely do not expect — give them a gift on their anniversary, hand them a $250 or $500 gift card, leave movie tickets on their desk, write a note that says, "Take the day off; you deserve it!" Or even send everyone in the office home on a beautiful, summer day — you are providing a memorable experience that is an essential component of delivering The Unexpected.

And delivering The Unexpected internally produces other effects — it enlivens your culture, builds loyalty, and subsequently causes your employees to say, "It's unbelievable what you do for me."

Memorable experiences are etched in your memory because they engender feelings of joy every time you recall them. As a result, when you deliver The Unexpected people more easily connect with you. Building your brand becomes a bit easier. And when those unexpected experiences lead to greater recognition from customers, vendors and employees, you tap into the viral nature of today's social media-driven society. And what better way to reach 6,000, 60,000 or even 600,000 people instead of simply six.

But as with anything, memorable experiences are memorable only because they're unique. This isn't like a traditional business technique. When you're dealing with The Unexpected, if you keep repeating what worked once or even twice, you can no longer expect it to be considered memorable. If it becomes routine, you'll move from delivering The Unexpected to simply delivering top-flight customer services — which isn't a bad thing. But if your goal is to deliver The Unexpected and achieve true separation from the competition, you must learn how to identify opportunities to do something really memorable.

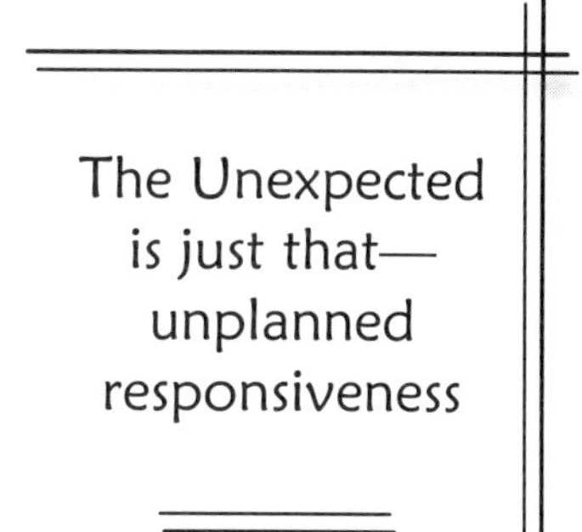

The great companies who ply The Unexpected empower their front-line employees to use creative judgment when it comes to creating memorable experiences. You can't set a corporate mandate to do something specific. Rather, the great ones give those front-line employees enough free reign to be innovative. And they understand that you don't need to do it every day to be considered great.

Remember Albertini's approach? Bringing the horse from Germany for Daimler's Zetsche may have cost her company about $10,000 or so, but the client loyalty and recognition it earned for her firm easily delivered a return of at least 10 times the financial investment because it was that memorable.

At The Ritz-Carlton, the reason delivering The Unexpected works so well is that they don't equate it specifically to set dollar amounts. They are simply seeking opportunities where doing something memorable resonates with their patrons and builds loyal fans. It is that extra step that allows them to charge a premium.

I honestly don't know for certain that when travelers stay at The Ritz-Carlton if they think they're going to be surprised each and every time by something memorable. But the point is that they've done it before, and that experiential event has built The Ritz-Carlton legend, so there's a widely held belief that staying at The Ritz-Carlton has the potential to turn into a memorable experience.

As I said earlier, nobody expects you to deliver the horse.

Creating something memorable can be done by anyone in any industry. To prove this, we've sought out numerous examples that illustrate The Unexpected in action.

"My experience with customers is that when you give them really unexpected service, it delivers something so memorable that they've never seen before, you have created a customer for life," explains Greg Dollarhyde, CEO of California-based Veggie Grill.

Dollarhyde knows a thing or two about building businesses by delivering memorable experiences. He previously served as chief executive and co-owner of the Baja Fresh Mexican Grill chain from 1998 to 2003, when he grew the chain from 30 to 250 units and then sold it to Wendy's International Inc. for $275 million. Dollarhyde is also the current executive chairman and the former CEO of Zoe's Kitchen, as well as executive chairman of Pacific Island Restaurants. He's developed a firm belief that when you learn how to deliver The Unexpected, you have a one-of-a-kind competitive advantage.

"We had this one time several years ago where one of our patrons had a terrible experience in one of our restaurants," Dollarhyde recalls. "We decided that giving them something like a free dessert just wasn't enough. So, one of our operations guys arranged for an entirely new dinner experience for the patron and some of his friends."

The manager had a limousine sent over to the man's house for him and four friends. They were taken to the restaurant, where the entire meal was on the house.

"We bought them dinner, drinks, anything they wanted," Dollarhyde says. "Then the limousine took them back home. The guys were completely surprised, and had one of the most memorable experiences in their lives. They couldn't wait to tell everyone they knew what we'd done."

Shrater, remembers an experience he had in 1995, while a student at The Wharton School of the University of Pennsylvania.

"I was a member of the solar car racing team," he recalls. "We were building a full-sized solar-powered car for a race, and we had purchased an $8,000 tracking system that had all these sensors for the vehicles and computerized gizmos for the pace car and our computers to track. With the system, we would have been able to see tire pressure, battery power, and all the relevant things going on with the vehicle."

As Shrater tells it, the system wasn't working properly. No matter what he and his classmates tried, they couldn't get it to function correctly. And they were getting desperate.

"It was a few days before the race," he says. "We were on the phone with the company in England that manufactured the product. And the service technician finally says, 'Our guy will be out there tomorrow to get it working for you.'"

Shrater says he expected that would be a local contractor or a U.S.-based partner who handled these types of problems, and that this person would drive down from wherever the closest location was in order to give him and his teammates a hand.

"Instead, they put a guy on a plane from England and flew him out to us," Shrater remembers. "He slept on a cot in somebody's dorm room and spent all day fixing the system and reprogramming it, on-site. Then, once it worked properly and we used it in the race, he flew back to England. That was unbelievable. And I think it says something that so many years later it still sticks with me."

That is the real challenge of delivering something memorable, explains Antisdel.

"You don't know what people expect and don't expect," he says. "To truly deliver The Unexpected it means taking a situation and going above and beyond to reach that exceptionally memorable experience."

Antisdel recalls an experience similar to his. "I was the CEO and one of the founders of a company called FurnitureFind. We had a customer who had ordered a dining room set from us and ordered it in plenty of time. But the manufacturer ran out of stock because something wasn't right in product and for some reason it wasn't going to ship on time.

"The dining room set was for the customer's daughter's wedding, and she bought it with the understanding that we would deliver it to her within six or eight weeks, well in time for the wedding, which was being held near Atlanta.

"This was probably a $7,000 dining room set," Antisdel says. "So we got a call from the manufacturer telling us they wouldn't be able to fulfill it, and we relayed that to the customer, who was obviously distressed. That's when we went into action."

Antisdel tasked his purchasing team with finding the exact dining room set in stock at another retailer's store, which they did.

"We bought it for her, picked it up and delivered it," Antisdel says. "We ended up paying significantly more for it than we were actually going to sell it to her for, but it was important for us to deliver upon the promise we made to the customer. To this day, she still talks about it. That's how memorable what we did was for her and her daughter's wedding."

Doing the memorable extends to the campuses of educational institutions — a place you normally wouldn't expect to see The Unexpected in action.

"It was orientation day for one of my university clients," says Bryan Golden, a business professional at the Culinary Institute of America and author of "Dare to Live Without Limits." "The director of residence life had brought me in to help. So I got there and he saw me. He came over and said, 'Sorry. I'm running a little behind. I'm helping the parents park their cars. If the parents find a parking space when they get here and bring their sons or daughters to college for the first time, they're happy. So give me a few more minutes before we sit down and talk.'

"I was literally blown away. Here was the director of residence life," Golden says, "who probably supervises hundreds of people throughout the college, out there helping parents park their cars, himself."

Even banks can do something memorable.

"When TD Bank was a bit smaller, they used to have lots of promotions," says Harlan Platt, a professor of finance at Northeastern University D'Amore-McKim School of Business. "One time, they were giving away a TD Bank clock thermometer shaped like a credit card. After I got it, I realized that my wife would love it because you could fold it up and take it around with you. So I went back to the bank and asked my banker if she could give me another for my wife."

Memorable experiences are those that occur outside of the normal interactions you have with an organization.

The banker returned and explained that unfortunately, they had run out of the clocks.

"I was a bit disappointed, but what could I do?" Platt says.

Weeks later, he went back to TD Bank for a routine visit and experienced The Unexpected.

"My banker saw me come in and disappeared into a back room," Platt recalls. "She came back and was holding something in her hand. She said, 'Here, I got this for your wife' and handed me a box with a clock in it." Platt was completely surprised. "She told me, 'We ran out, but I tracked down the original prototype.' That was so unexpected, so memorable, that I'll never forget it. And every time I see that clock I think about why we bank at TD Bank."

8 Be Distinguishable and Your Brand Will Benefit

Delivering a memorable experience — even one that delights and surprises — is not enough to break free from the overly crowded marketplace. Sure, you may cause a stir once, or even twice. But even Walmart, with its commoditized products and sterile, big box format, knows how to deliver a memorable experience every now and again. To truly raise your game to the next level, you must learn how to leverage memorable experiences and transform them into brand-building opportunities that differentiate you from your competition.

Executed correctly, you accomplish the second element needed to successfully deliver The Unexpected — creating a brand that is distinguishable.

Why is being distinguishable so important? Strictly speaking, because while providing the "memorable" etches an experience in someone's mind, being distinguishable makes people think about your brand. And when your company's brand is at the top of the list — or the only name on the list — for times when a customer wants to be surprised and delighted, the benefit to your organization is immeasurable.

"We were doing business with EarthLink on a new venture in East Africa and Kenya and our company was trying to get the project off the ground," remembers Mark Wilson, the former CEO of Atlanta-based teleservices and outsourced customer service contact firm Ryla. "It has its share of complications. So I went to Africa to be with the customer to ensure the project was completed. I could have sent a project manager, but I wanted to oversee this myself. In my mind, it wasn't enough to satisfy the customer, I wanted to be sure the project's success was at a level where Ryla would earn a customer for life."

So Wilson spent two straight days and nights — a combined 48 hours — with the client, monitoring the progress and troubleshooting.

"I literally went back to my hotel to shower and change only a few times, and then returned to oversee the launch of this from start to finish," Wilson says.

During the process, the client was surprised that Wilson, the CEO, was overseeing the project himself rather than assigning it to a project manager and waiting for field reports on the initiative's progress.

"When we were done, I knew I'd cemented our reputation firmly in the customer's heads so that they wouldn't consider looking somewhere else the next time," says Wilson. "When it came to what our reputation was because of this, it put us ahead of our competitors and separated us from everyone else."

From Wilson's perspective, his ability to deliver The Unexpected forever distinguished Ryla's brand — not just with EarthLink executives but for executives of any organization who heard about the initiative.

A 10-percent increase in customer retention levels result in a 30-percent increase in the value of the company.
Source: Bain & Co.

To be truly distinguishable, you must be able to move the needle solidly away from other brands and toward yours. Your own delivery of The Unexpected needs to provide an experiential moment or unique service that becomes so memorable, so different, from anything the recipient has received or experience up until that moment that your brand suddenly becomes elevated from another "Guess what happened to me this one time..." to a non-negotiable "must buy" every time there could be options on whom to use.

Being distinguishable is critically important in hospitality, where dozens, if not hundreds, of brands battle it out for travelers to choose from. With so much at stake, what's to differentiate one specific port of lodging from another?

Because of that, there are literally dozens of examples of what hotels are doing to draw attention to themselves. But it is how hotels ply innovative services to deliver The Unexpected to travelers and guests in pursuit of building loyalty and creating buzz that separates the true heavyweights from the pretenders. Among them is Dallas-based Rosewood Hotels and Resorts, which in January 2012 began offering a 24-hour Fragrance Butler at several of its luxury properties across the world.

At the time, Rosewood described the service as an opportunity it had identified because of skyrocketing checked baggage fees and strict Transportation Security Administration regulations limiting liquids in carry-ons. Rosewood's solution to the problem it identified — traveling with one's signature colognes or perfumes had become increasingly challenging and often expensive — was both innovative and distinguishable.

The program allows guests to ring a Fragrance Butler at any time — day or night. The butler arrives at the guest's door carrying a silver tray with 10 high-end fragrances for guests' use. The guest selects a fragrance, mists him or herself, and then the Fragrance Butler leaves.

While providing additional amenities isn't completely unexpected for travelers — even high-end amenities — Rosewood's solution went one step further. The chain distinguished itself from other luxury chains by aligning its Fragrance Butler service with its A Sense of Place® philosophy, which was designed to embrace the local cultures of each property's physical location.

As a result, each of Rosewood's city properties features a distinctly unique fragrance menu — offering Hermès Eau des Merveilles at The Carlyle in New York City, Givenchy Dahlia Noir at Rosewood Mansion on Turtle Creek in Dallas, Tom Ford Black Orchid at the Rosewood Hotel Georgia in Vancouver and Bassem Al Qassem Geneva at Al Faisaliah Hotel in Riyadh, Saudi Arabia.

Or consider this experience recounted by a *Fortune* 500 company executive after a near-disaster threatened to disrupt an important recruiting event.

A few years ago, Parker Hannifin, a 58,000-employee, $13 billion public company based in Cleveland, that manufactures motion and control technologies, was hosting several job candidates at the Cleveland Marriott East, a hotel that in 2010 ranked the 23rd best property out of Marriott's 338 branded hotels and resorts in North America because of its team's commitment to identifying new ways to stretch its service.

Parker Hannifin seeks out the best and brightest engineers to staff its 300-plus locations worldwide. And it is constantly in recruiting mode. It was a typical terrible Northeast Ohio winter day, which made for challenging travel from the hotel to Parker Hannifin's global headquarters.

"Our scheduled shuttle bus didn't arrive at the hotel on Tuesday morning, Feb. 1st," writes Mike Klein, Parker Hannifin's college recruiting manager and learning and development manager, Sales & Marketing. "The transportation company was not able to provide a replacement vehicle in a reasonable amount of time."

Klein knew that shuttling all the candidates back and forth from the hotel to Parker Hannifin's headquarters in the two cars he had on hand would be a grueling and arduous task. With the weather working against him, it would take hours and put the recruiting event's schedule in jeopardy. But there weren't many other choices available to Klein and his team.

Suddenly, Cleveland Marriott East's general manager surprised Klein. He noticed the situation and without prodding offered Klein the use of his personal vehicle. He also contacted a personal friend who lived near the hotel who owned a large SUV. Within a very short period of time, everyone was mobile again. Between Klein's and the two improvised vehicles from the hotel, the group was able to transport every candidate staying at the

Marriott to Parker Hannifin's corporate headquarters and prevented any major delays with the recruiting event.

Writes Klein, "Their service is what brings me back to the Cleveland Marriott East."

But even being distinguishable, as with anything connected to The Unexpected, there's a warning worth heeding: You can't plan your entire strategy around it or else what you deliver will become what's expected, says Bitner.

For example, if Rosewood failed to continue to innovate beyond the Fragrance Butler, or if the team at Cleveland Marriott East wasn't trained to identify and react to opportunities to elevate their game, their services would become yet another high-end offering for what are already considered upper echelon brands. There would be nothing distinguishable about them.

"These organizations," says Bitner, "the ones that are consistently known for their world-class customer service and doing unexpected things, they're also cutting edge. Consistent unexpected service could really be described as innovation because these are companies that keep looking at new, innovative ways to deliver for their customer. It definitely differentiates them from others in their industry. And when you're distinguishable, you build customer loyalty and traffic, which clearly enhances your brand.

9 When The Unexpected Goes Viral

Few things delight entrepreneurs or CEOs more than seeing positive news about their companies' products or services spread like wildfire through the masses, reaching millions of current and potential customers via the tremendous power and influence of social media.

The reality, however, is that no matter how hard you try — or how much you want or wish it to happen — you cannot force something to make the move from "shared online" to "globally viral." But that doesn't mean the experiences you deliver to your customers, vendors and employees can't — or won't — go viral in their own way. In fact, the more memorable the experience — good or bad — the greater chance that news of it will reach larger numbers of people.

"Social media is a weapon," Busse says. "It is a weapon because you can have customer interaction with an employee from your company and, within seconds, someone can tweet about it, putting comments up on Facebook, and in minutes the whole world will know about the situation. Social media can be an organization's worst nightmare ... or free advertising."

One of the starkest realities, Busse says, is that businesses today are always under the microscope. Social media's unique dynamic — instant communication — has altered the landscape of business. Now, it is easy to share every story about every experience you provide for your customers, prospects and employees.

This is a dramatic difference from the days when if you had an experience that was memorable and distinguishable that you'd relish telling one or two people at a time. If you had the opportunity, you'd expand that story to an entire group of maybe six or seven.

Everywhere you look these days, the signs point to the same conclusion — we live in a viral society. And the speed at which information is disseminated through social media is downright frightening.

> "If you do build a great experience, customers tell each other about that. Word of mouth is very powerful."
> —Jeff Bezos, CEO, Amazon.com

Busse has a simple solution to this brave, new world: "If you want better stories," she says, "provide better experiences."

At the same time as this dramatic sea change, consumers also are becoming more dependent on searching online for an organization's reputation before doing business with them. Services such as Indianapolis-based Angie's List have built entire operations on the growing truism that what people say about you online will make or break your business. Now, each and every touch point is an opportunity to take a positive or negative story about your organization and reach millions of people.

As the gravitas of social media becomes more apparent each day, executives are growing increasingly powerless. They watch complaints about them become the video de jour on YouTube, emerge as a trending topic on Twitter and elicit an avalanche of comments on Facebook — all of which somehow originated from a single post or mention on a blog or someone's personal page.

The simple fact is that leaders who ignore the viral nature of their organizations' service interactions and fail to deal with their customers, clients and vendors properly are destined to face a backlash from the public, as well as earn a bad reputation. Neglect can be much more harmful to a company's brand than almost anything else.

One of the first organizations to learn this painful lesson was United Airlines, which faced its own nightmare when Dave Carroll's "United Breaks Guitars" video became an Internet sensation and was seen by more than 150 million people worldwide.

In 2008, Carroll, a Canadian musician, and his band, Sons of Maxwell, were travelling to Omaha, Nebraska, from Halifax, Nova Scotia. Carroll had checked his Taylor guitar with United Airlines — it was too big and bulky to be a carry-on item.

During a layover at Chicago O'Hare International Airport, Carroll heard a fellow passenger say that baggage handlers were "throwing guitars" outside the plane.

He alerted three flight attendants, who Carroll says, "showed complete indifference toward me."

In Omaha, he confirmed his worst fears and found his was guitar broken.

Carroll's battle with the airlines to take responsibility for its employees' actions led to the creation and release of his music video. The video's viral nature, with its haunting chorus, "United breaks guitars," caused a subsequent public relations nightmare for United.

Stories like Carroll's would have been forced off the front page a few years ago by a series of strong positive public relations campaigns. But today, lip service is no longer enough. Because viral videos like Carroll's remain online seemingly forever, companies need to go even further — instituting significant structural changes to their policies and procedures.

But it doesn't have to be this way. Going viral doesn't always need to be a negative experience. When it comes to relaying stories of organizations that deliver The Unexpected, there can be a just as significant positive effect created — assuming you recognize the power of social media and are willing to embrace it.

"Social media has offered us a golden opportunity to engage with our customers and offer a new level of customer service," writes the management team of Rackspace on its website. "Our 'Rackers' can respond through various channels such as LinkedIn to offer advice and resolve issues."

Innovative thinking like this allows any company to offer expanded levels of support for customers. For Rackspace, it meant being nominated for and receiving numerous awards for customer service, including the National Customer Service Award in 2009 and 2010.

Further, Rackspace management recognized that surprising and delighting its audience had tremendous benefits for the company. They understood how a happy feeling instilled by an unexpected service offering could cause the recipient to take a few seconds to hammer out a few, "I can't believe what just happened to me ..." lines on his or her smartphone, iPad or laptop and share it with the world.

Better yet, depending on the sophistication and following of the person sharing the message through social networks — as well as the right set of identifiers and tags — the wheels could be set in motion for a truly viral experience.

"It (social media) takes what historically has been behavior we all have done offline, and when you bring it online and digitize it, it starts to scale and moves at a speed with which we haven't seen previously," explains LinkedIn CEO Jeff Weiner. "It really has the opportunity to change everything it touches."

Just as important, as your company's service experiences go viral, you must recognize that your organization no longer has the exclusive ability to determine the shape and tenor of the message being delivered.

"It really is an issue of control," says Gina Bianchini, founder of Ning.com and entrepreneur-in-residence at Andreessen-Horowitz, a Menlo Park, California-based venture capital firm. "That's probably the biggest cultural sea change that we as business leaders need to deal with. We are used to running an ad on page six in a magazine or filming a TV commercial, and you run it on a network and that's really the beginning and the end."

But having what you do go viral results in relinquished control.

"The consumers now control you," she says. "And I think we need to be prepared to completely be involved in those social conversations. We need to be able to monitor them. We need to be able to respond to them. And, perhaps the biggest change for those of us who are running businesses where discipline is like customer service or mission critical, getting to somebody's question or somebody's issue 'sometime' is no longer acceptable. We now have to be able to manage that in real time. That's probably the biggest change for those of us who are evolving from more traditional to sort of 2.0, 3.0 businesses."

Today, with social media networks such as Pinterest, Twitter, Yelp, Foursquare, Facebook and Google Plus dictating how we interact with others, understanding the viral impact of The Unexpected is critical when your primary goal is effective competition.

Here's a simple experiment any organization can try as proof. Log on to any social network and monitor a series of keywords relating to customer service.

What comes up when that happens? Most likely, you see people talking about what's happened to them — good or bad.

Now, eliminate the conversations about the bad experiences and focus on the good ones.

As you read them, does the passion and emotion surrounding how enjoyable those positive, unexpected experiences transfer to you? Do they create some sort of belief that you want to experience these yourself?

Not surprisingly, you most likely will feel something positive. That's because when people talk through social media about doing The Unexpected, people take notice and want to experience it themselves.

When you put this into context for a business owner, leader or entrepreneur, the stakes can rise even higher. Depending on your industry, customer acquisition costs can run very high, and they often have a lengthy closing cycle. Anything you're able to do to shorten that cycle and reduce acquisition costs has a positive impact on your bottom line.

So when a viral story about your company surrounds an incident of you delivering The Unexpected, what do you think will happen?

Because you've differentiated yourself from the competition, that memorable and distinguishable experience has the ability to assume a life of its own. People will talk about your organization and the experiences you provide. Those weighing in are greater in number than those who have personally experienced it, and this new population also includes people who want to experience it themselves. Better yet, because the shelf life of information online is considerably longer than one-to-one communication, there's a good chance the message will continue to be passed along for months, if not years, and take on legendary status.

By delivering The Unexpected, the net result is that your brand gets stronger and your reach longer. Going viral allows you to reach the masses because of your ability to identify opportunities to deliver memorable and distinguishable experiences.

10 Memorable + Distinguishable + Viral = Profitable

Consumers want to interact with truly exceptional organizations. Customer loyalty is predicated on being the first place people turn to when they need what you offer. The importance of developing and maintaining a stable of steady, repeat customers cannot be overemphasized. On average, 80 percent of any company's profit comes from 20 percent of its customers, so finding scalable ways to create repeat business is a bit like having a magic elixir.

Further, when you provide distinguishable service that delivers surprise and delight through memorable experiences, you can often render price irrelevant. And when price is removed from purchasing decisions, the door opens to commanding premium pricing.

Understandably, not every organization can fulfill both elements because many companies play in spaces where the price for their products has been severely commoditized. For those who are able to command premium pricing, however, the rewards are that much greater.

Dollarhyde doesn't compete through premium pricing at Veggie Grill. Instead, he believes creating loyal and repeat customers is the answer to fostering Veggie Grill's growth. Dollarhyde's team focuses on providing customer experiences so memorable that the recipients can't help but tell others about them. They also come back again and again to find out what might happen next.

An example of how Veggie Grill delivers The Unexpected is Veggie Grill's Birthday Club. Visitors to the restaurant chain's website or customers who go into the store are invited to register for the club. The pitch informs potential registrants, "Let us send you something for your birthday."

That "something" turns out to be a free meal on the person's birthday — not a bad trade for providing an email address and agreeing to receive an email newsletter. But it's not an example of The Unexpected. That arrives next. This is where Dollarhyde's ability to deliver The Unexpected separates Veggie Grill from its competitors.

When your birthday rolls around, Veggie Grill sends more than a free birthday meal. It includes another offer: Let us know if you're working on your birthday, and we'll make lunch for you and a few of your friends

That, in itself, is a good example of The Unexpected. But wait, Veggie Grill goes even further.

After the birthday celebrant picks up free lunch, there is another surprise inside the bag — free lunch cards, inviting everyone to return to the restaurant for yet another free meal.

Explains Dollarhyde, "That's really unexpected service, and people are quite blown away by it. They think, 'Wow, this restaurant can do this. What else can they do?' And all we're trying to do is get our food in people's mouths so that they realize how good the food is, come back in and try it again and again.

"We want them to talk about it with their friends. And we want them to get on social networks to talk about it with the masses. At that point, our effort to deliver a completely different level of customer service turns into something highly profitable."

Veggie Grill's concept for delivering The Unexpected can be adapted to nearly any industry where it's possible to send prospects free introductory samples. Those can be wrapped in memorable experiences and used to convert prospects into loyal customers. And for those organizations that offer products and services that can be positioned to command premium prices, the combination of loyal customers and premium prices makes the profitability ceiling even higher.

This dynamic has never been more important than it is today. Too many businesses are mired in a no-win race to be crowned their industry's low-cost provider. Mastering The Unexpected will change that game and help break the cycle of depressed pricing. Done correctly, you will no longer be forced to watch your profit margin painfully erode.

Think back to the first time you heard about Starbucks or walked in and saw the prices. If you are like most people, you initially questioned why anyone in their right mind would pay $4 to $5 for a cup of coffee and maybe thought of the fast-food restaurant down the street selling coffee for $1 a cup with free refills. You may have also wondered how Starbucks was able to generate any repeat business.

Then you looked around. You saw the customers who used Starbucks as a meeting place or de facto office. You heard the music playing over the store's audio system; it was something different, new. You watched the baristas transform the process of ordering and making coffee into an experience — going as far as coming up with creative names for the personalized concoctions. And then, suddenly, you realized the brilliance and simplicity of Schultz's business model.

Research confirms his ideas. Consumers in an American Express survey conducted in 2011 said they would spend an average of 13 percent more money with companies that provided excellent service. And it's hard to knock the service you consistently receive at Starbucks.

So how can you follow Schultz's lead and command premium prices for your own products and services?

Start by recognizing it's not enough to think price first. Beginning with a higher-priced product or service and then hoping that everything else just falls into place is a trap many anxious entrepreneurs fall into in their quest to create a business with a hefty profit margin.

Executives who lead with price often end up with unsustainable business models doomed to fail. Consider how many trendy, overly expensive restaurants have come and gone in just the past five years. And think about why staffing high-end retail stores with front-line employees who have long-outdated superiority complexes and act snobbish toward prospective customers who don't look as though they have American Express Platinum cards is a terrible foundation for a culture supposedly built to deliver The Unexpected.

Greater profitability through premium pricing comes from successfully executing the three other elements of The Unexpected — creating customer experiences that are memorable, being distinguishable from the competition, and having word spread from customers to prospects by being viral.

> The revenue impact from a 10 percentage point improvement in a company's customer experience score can translate into more than $1 billion.
> Source: Forrester Business Impact of Customer Experience

When you are able to remove price as a purchasing decision factor and focus on service, commanding a premium where it is appropriate will dramatically increase your profit margin. Three in five people in the American Express survey said they would try new brands or companies after a bad experience in hopes of finding something better. Nearly 80 percent said they had abandoned planned purchases due to subpar customer service experiences. In every case, price was never mentioned as a factor.

Further, there are significant opportunities for organizations of all sizes to benefit from embracing the idea of delivering The Unexpected. Six in 10 Americans said they believed businesses in general had not done a good job of increasing their focus on providing good service, and a majority of respondents believed small companies place a larger emphasis on customer service.

And as with everything tied to customer service, one of the keys to profitability is recognizing that employees who interact with customers every day are the real brand ambassadors for any company. How employees treat customers and create memorable experiences provides a direct correlation to the pricing level that can be set for products and services — especially when that company is not an industry that competes solely on price.

This is why nearly every company that successfully delivers The Unexpected points to its front-line team members as the reason why they are able to do what they do.

"Our primary focus is on hiring the right people and just letting them be themselves," says Aaron Magness, marketer at Betabrand and former senior director of brand marketing and business development at Zappos.com. "We hire people that are committed to providing great customer service."

Jane Judd, senior manager of Zappos' customer loyalty team, manages those front-line people.

"In order to build a brand you have to have a culture first," she says. "Once you have the culture, everything falls in place. Our front-line people are some of our best brand advocates. And in the contact center, we are trying to build loyalty. On any given day, 75 percent of our customers are loyal, repeat customers. So we try to go that extra mile and build that relationship, which translates into loyalty … and repeat business."

And Zappos goes one step further to ensure its team is comprised of service-oriented members: It offers new hires $2,000 to quit if they are not fully committed to the company.

Jim FitzGibbon, president of worldwide hotel operations for Four Seasons Hotels and Resorts, agrees that success rests with having the right type people in place.

"We believe the key to delivering a great guest experience is listening and building the confidence of the employees to respond to the needs of the customer in a unique way every time," he says.

FitzGibbon, as well as other leaders at Four Seasons, understands that people who choose to pay premium pricing for a hotel such as Four

Seasons, expect more. That higher expectation comes with an acceptance that you can't really drop the ball and hope to recover it later.

"Now that more and more people choose to interact and share through social media networks, for example, not only do we have to listen in a different way, but the experience itself extends beyond the face-to-face interaction," he says. "Whether at our hotels and resorts or online, having employees who feel empowered to embody the service excellence our brand stands for remains top priority."

That extra step organizations that deliver The Unexpected take, allows them to charge a premium and be more profitable. Consumers may not believe they're going to be surprised in every interaction, but there is an unspoken recognition that your organization has done it before. And that experience, which was so memorable, has created the feeling that yours is an unbelievable company and whatever you charge, it's worth it.

"People will pay a premium for service quality, and they will do that if they believe they're getting value and it's consistent over time," Bitner says. "Our research over the past 15 to 20 years indicates that's pretty well shown. But this only works if it's consistent, innovative, done over a longer period of time and doesn't seem like it's just another flash in the pan."

And better yet, Bitner's research has found that there is no correlation between how much money you must spend to deliver the type of unexpected customer service that allows you to be highly profitable.

"A lot of times people think that service has to be costly," she says. "But many of the things people are looking for aren't costly. It doesn't require a big investment to be courteous and provide consistent service. A lot of it simply depends on the training and development of people."

Part Two

The Unexpected In Action—Any Industry, Any Time, Any Size

11 Develop Legendary Stories That Others Will Tell For You

Few other companies worldwide have invested so much into establishing its customer-service legend than Nordstrom. As we've discussed earlier in the book, Nordstrom eats, sleeps and breathes customer service — or at least it certainly seems that way. What matters, however, is that Nordstrom's culture thrives on its employees' passion to deliver memorable experiences for customers and, in the process, create the next viral story. And, its brilliance comes from not micromanaging how those stories are told, instead relying on its customers — and others — to pass along those legendary stories on Nordstrom's behalf.

Stories of The Unexpected at Nordstrom are ubiquitous; speak with any Nordstrom customer or employee, and you'll find someone actively in search of either creating or experiencing their own legend. We spoke with customers, employees, read news articles and scoured blogs to see what makes Nordstrom tick. The stories can — and do — fill books. I've included one that I believe best illustrates how Nordstrom employees embody that "eyes up" philosophy espoused by Zane, and strive to identify and act upon opportunities to deliver The Unexpected.

On the last day of her vacation in Chicago, Jan found a neat, little boutique that sold attractive pants that fit her well. After purchasing the pants, Jan realized she and her friends were running late for their flight home to Florida. They packed their bags, rushed to the airport and caught their flight.

The next morning, Jan excitedly put on her pants only to learn that the security tag was still on one of the pant legs. Her discovery put a damper on Jan's excitement and she immediately called the store in Chicago to see what could be done.

The salesperson who had sold her the pants was empathetic. She apologized to Jan, told her to send them back, and assured her she would take care of removing the tag and send them back to Jan in Florida.

Jan wasn't satisfied. After all, she wanted to wear her new pants, and she asked whether there was anything else that could be done to rectify the situation in a shorter period of time.

The salesperson couldn't think of one, and told Jan she could send the pants back for a full refund if she so desired.

Jan thought about it. But more important, she thought about the pants and how much she liked how they fit. She decided to call her local Nordstrom in South Florida to see if they had those exact pants in stock.

The saleswoman checked and found that the store did, indeed, have those pants in stock. But rather than try to sell her the new pair of pants, she suggested that Jan bring the original pants into the store and she would take the security tag off.

Jan, a little shocked, quickly explained that she hadn't bought the pants at Nordstrom. But the salesperson was undeterred, saying that wasn't a problem at all. When Jan arrived at the store later that day, a salesperson was waiting for her to remove the security tag.

Moments later, a member of Nordstrom's loss prevention team returned and said the tag on her pants was not the type that Nordstrom's used nor had the equipment to safely remove. An alert saleswoman, however, intercepted the pants, and with a smile said, "I think Saks has this type of tag on it. I'll be right back."

Before Jan could respond, the saleswoman rushed out of the store. Shortly after, she returned, pants in hand, security tag removed.

The sheer number of similar stories from Nordstrom customers makes it certain that each retelling adds a new level of legendary, "You won't believe what happened at Nordstrom ..." to it.

What is it that makes Nordstrom so special in the realm of customer service?

First and foremost, Nordstrom, as an organization and as a group of employees, lives the legend and seeks to expand upon it. Since its founding in 1901 as a simple shoe store, Nordstrom has been guided by its founder's philosophy to offer customers the best possible service, selection, quality and value.

> "The goal as a company is to have customer service that is not just the best but legendary."
> —Sam Walton, founder, Walmart

This passion extends to every in-person interaction. When you walk into any store, you'll find that every register has a pen and paper available for customers to share their individual stories.

And continuing the service-oriented storytelling companywide is more than just encouraged. In fact, every morning, before each store opens, employees assemble in the main lobby where the store manager shares some of the best stories from the previous day and rewards the employees in those stores who contributed to the experiences.

The simplicity of this idea is amazing — by bringing together and celebrating delivery of The Unexpected, Nordstrom's management team has created a culture where employees actively think about the next way they're going to deliver a memorable experience to customers.

Does Nordstrom sometimes drop the ball and make mistakes? Is every interaction with Nordstrom worthy of the legend? Of course not. But that's the power of delivering The Unexpected. It transcends everything else.

Let's take a closer look at Jan's story, as well as how Nordstrom views its world-class customer service and reinforces it to employees, and see how anyone can apply the ideas.

Jan's story, like numerous others from the Nordstrom legend box, are clearly Memorable — not just for the recipient, but for every man, woman and child who hears about it. Tales of Nordstrom's ability to deliver The Unexpected are etched in our memories, so much so that when you hear the words "customer service" and "retail" in the same breath, the example that comes to mind is nearly always Nordstrom. Because of that, the brand has become Distinguishable from every other retailer on the planet.

Powered by the stories and the brand, Nordstrom is probably the most Viral retailer around. As of the summer of 2014, more than 2.7 million people like Nordstrom on Facebook and nearly half a million people worldwide follow its Twitter feed. The conversations across social media — as well as the tens of thousands of images "pinned" to its pages on Pinterest — only serve to reinforce the legend.

Nordstrom also excels in both areas of being Profitable: Its brand is powerful enough to allow Nordstrom to command premium pricing on many of its products and services in its main stores; and the company has consistently reported profitable quarters year after year since the devastating economic downturn of 2008.

Further, the organization spends considerable time and money training its team members to be cognizant of opportunities to deliver unexpected customer service to customers whenever possible, and each day not only celebrates stories of The Unexpected but also rewards employees who are involved in creating those memorable experiences.

Just because Nordstrom has the considerable financial muscle and acuity to accomplish delivery of The Unexpected doesn't mean that other, smaller organizations can't follow suit.

The key to providing Nordstrom-style service is that the goal to deliver it must come from the top down, and this is where it's essential that management teams lead by example and achieve buy-in from employees on the front line.

One of the things that Sam Walton, founder of Walmart, did during his early days was spend much of his time in the stores. He walked around with a clipboard and talked to people. And there were only two groups of people that Walton wanted to speak with: customers and the people directly serving the customers.

"That was brilliant in its simplicity," Golden says. "Those two groups told Walton everything he needed to know about his business — what he was doing right and what he was doing wrong."

And, when it comes to developing legendary stories that others will tell for you, anything that builds a vocal, loyal fan base that's active on social media will help you on your way toward achieving success.

Some savvy organizations have even gone so far as incorporating big data into their ability to create those legendary stories. If you're a golfer, or even just a fan of the game, you have no doubt heard stories about the famous Firestone Country Club, which has hosted three PGA championships and is the permanent home of the World Golf Championships-Bridgestone Invitational.

Part of the ClubCorp family of golf club properties, beyond its amazing golf courses, Firestone is well-known for wowing its members and guests with daily instances of The Unexpected.

Every person who attends Firestone is considered a VIP — and they have the stories to prove it. Staff members are trained to seek out opportunities to deliver surprise and delight. Their goal is to create a memorable experience, distinguish the club from other golf clubs, and keep people saying, "You won't believe what happened to me at Firestone."

Upon arrival, everyone — guests and members, alike — are greeted by name, and the staff considers it friendly competition to find ways to outdo each other in delivering personal touches throughout the visit. Items such as personal, handwritten letters and welcome gifts are put into lockers for members and guests, set on golf carts and placed in overnight rooms. Every guest also finds his or her name on his or her respective locker.

Empowered team members deliver The Unexpected in a variety of ways:

- One server brought in her personal stock of Diet Coke because the club only carries Pepsi products. She noticed guests asking for Diet Coke and decided to act.
- A group once held their corporate golf outing on the same day as the final round of the U.S. Open. The director of maintenance noticed the overlap, taped the match, and it replayed during the group's cocktails and hors d'oeuvres later that evening.
- When a member once made a birthday dinner reservation, the assistant service directors knew a key fact about him: He loved key lime pie. Even though the club didn't offer that type of pie on the menu, they rushed off to a store, bought a key lime pie, and had it delivered to the guest's table after dinner, creating a memorable experience he would never forget.
- On one particularly cloudy day, sensing it would rain, the event marketing and sales director walked through the parking lot and noticed one of the club's members had left his convertible top down. The team member found out what course the man was playing on, tracked him down, collected his keys, and rushed back to put the car top up for him — just as it started to rain.

We identified scores of examples where Firestone team members delivered The Unexpected for guests and members. All of them were due to a meticulous focus on wanting to surprise people who visit the club — and the recipients weren't shy to recount the stories over and over to anyone who would listen.

Achieving this level of unexpected delivery isn't easy. Firestone has developed several systems that assist staff members in their quest to serve members better — but all of them are processes any organization could implement and apply in their own ways.

One is Firestone's master database, MemberPride, which keeps track of all member contact information, birthdays, anniversaries, interests, educational and professional background, family information, and general demographics. It helps Firestone staff members get to know its nearly 1,000 members and personalize the service they receive.

Another tool is Dashboard, which tracks member usage and visits. That information provides critical trend-related information that team members can tap into and use.

> An unexpected reward fires a dopamine circuit and tells the brain to pay attention.

At the beginning of each day, internal emails are sent around to every employee to make them aware of what events are occurring that day, which members will be attending them, who is checking in, and what members have birthdays that day.

Each department holds lineups at the start of every shift. At them, staff members are informed about the day's events and review who is at the club that day. Firestone has even created a member picture profile book for each department. Each member is listed in it with his or her picture, name, member numbers and the company for which they work.

Firestone's hiring process is a tough one. Applicants must pass the select test, which tests them on ethics and customer service instincts. All department applicants must also pass the assess test, which determines if they have the necessary leadership and management aptitude qualities to succeed at the club. Only those applicants who pass the tests are moved to the next step of the application process — rounds of in-depth interviews that weed out personalities that don't fit the club's culture.

For those who are service-oriented enough for Firestone's high standards, training begins on day one. New employees are enrolled in a program called Right Start, which teaches customer service values and goal, and trains staff members on how to put those philosophies into practice. They are also trained in Firestone's 3 Steps of Service: warm welcomes, magic moments and fond farewells.

The warm welcome includes recognizing every guest by name. Employees strive to be the first to use the guest's name and say, "Hello, how can I help you?" Or, "How are you doing today?" Even today, people are surprised and remember when you use their names.

Magic moments describe staff members' random acts of kindness. They actively seek out opportunities to deliver The Unexpected. Firestone's belief is that delivering The Unexpected infuses energy, fun and excitement across the entire club. They become the basis for most of the legendary stories about Firestone that people tell.

Finally, fond farewells should leave a lasting impression on the guest so that they are encouraged to return and tell stories about their experience. When team members do this, Firestone's legacy continues.

> Over 1 million people view tweets about customer service every week. Roughly 80 percent of those tweets are negative or critical in nature.

Stories are powerful things. They are what people remember. And when you're able to get other people to tell those stories over and over again on your organization's behalf they bring The Unexpected to life — and can power your organization to rise above the competition.

12 Anticipate Customer Needs and Deliver Memorable Experiences

There is a commonly held myth that when it comes to customer service, larger organizations with deeper pockets maintain a significant advantage over their smaller brethren.

This theory relies on the notion that larger entities can — and will — devote greater resources to delivering world-class service to their customers: more employees in a service center, more complex service systems and perhaps they may even integrate enterprise-level software to manage the entire customer service process.

But despite any financial advantages a larger organization may possess, when it comes to delivering The Unexpected to consumers, in many cases having more dollars to spend doesn't provide any advantage. Rather, what makes a difference among organizations is a nonfinancial factor — having the desire to deliver memorable service that provides surprise and delight, differentiates your organization and gets people to talk about you. And, the smaller the organization, the more apt they are to use the resources they have on hand to identify any competitive advantage they can muster.

When you desire to find ways to deliver The Unexpected — and commit to training your team to learn how to identify opportunities to make it happen — you level the playing field against the competition in ways that money simply can't buy. But you must make this belief part of your organization's DNA — and part of it is being able to anticipate your customers' needs and deliver memorable experiences that they'll never forget.

The Ritz-Carlton, as we discussed earlier, has mastered this process. Tales of The Ritz-Carlton's ability to deliver The Unexpected are nearly as ubiquitous as those of The Walt Disney Co.

One family staying at The Ritz-Carlton, Bali, had carried specialized eggs and milk for their son who suffered from food allergies. After they arrived, the family realized the eggs had broken and the milk had soured.

At the direction of the hotel manager, the dining staff searched the city but was unable to find the appropriate items. Then the executive chef remembered a store in Singapore that sold them. He contacted his mother-in-law, who lived in Singapore, asked her to buy the products and then fly to Bali to deliver them, nearly 1,500 miles away. His mother-in-law agreed. The lengths to which The Ritz-Carlton staff went to ensure a memorable experience surprised the family.

In April 2010, at The Ritz-Carlton, Cleveland, the brother of a future guest called to ask Guest Recognition Coordinator Bernadette Csizek if he could pay for a stay his brother and sister were planning at the hotel. He wanted to surprise them by picking up the bill.

The brother went on to explain that his sister-in-law was very ill and battling cancer, and that his brother and she had planned some quiet time together so that they could try to relax and temporarily distance themselves from the medical issues they were facing.

Csizek accepted the advance payment from the brother and shared the story with Front Office Manager Michelle Thomas. They decided to work together to create a series of unexpected delights that would make the couple's stay as relaxing and special as they could — without causing a distracting commotion.

They bought flowers for the couple's room, and set up chilled bottles of champagne and sparkling grape juice for them to enjoy. An assortment of chocolate-covered strawberries and fresh mixed berries were also laid out.

When the guests arrived, Csizek and Thomas personally met them at the front desk and delivered the keys to their room. The couple entered their room and found rose petals and candles. Flowers were on the desk; the champagne and berries were nearby. There was even another bag of rose petals in the bathroom in case the wife wanted to take a hot, relaxing bath.

When the couple checked out, Csizek and Thomas presented them with a gift — a picture frame inscribed with the phrase, "Memories are not something you have … they are something you treasure."

Needless to say, the entire experience created something memorable that clearly distinguished The Ritz-Carlton from other luxury hotel chains.

But not everything The Ritz-Carlton does to deliver The Unexpected is planned. In fact, The Ritz-Carlton encourages its team members — called Ladies and Gentlemen — to seek out opportunities to spontaneously deliver memorable surprise and delight. And every Lady and Gentleman is empowered to act on his or her own when the opportunity arises.

For example, if staff members notice a guest tends to sleep on the right side of the bed, but the room's alarm clock and iPod docking station is located on the left side, they take it upon themselves to change the environment to make the guest more comfortable.

"Customer service is the experience we deliver to our customer. It's the promise we keep to the customer. It's how we follow through for the customer. It's how we make them feel when they do business with us."
—Shep Hyken, author, *The Amazement Revolution*

It doesn't take much for any organization's employees to identify this type of opportunity — it's not much more than paying attention to how people act and their preferences.

The Ritz-Carlton's Ladies and Gentlemen are also trained to anticipate guests' needs. If a team member notices a guest orders only Diet Coke when dining at The Ritz-Carlton, they may arrange for a Diet Coke to be poured and brought over to the table prior to his or her request. More than once, a team member has decided to have a personalized beverage amenity in an incoming guest's room, awaiting his or her arrival.

Through The Ritz-Carlton's detailed training regimen, management has built a team of employees who understand how to perceive, empathize, anticipate and respond to guests. This group recognizes the simple fact that if they are able to share something in meaningful ways with those they meet, they will create a legendary experience that will be communicated to others.

In the hospitality business, where The Ritz-Carlton competes, being able to focus on others can mean the difference between success and failure. And this is what many other industries are beginning to realize as their own competition increases. It's the main reason why The Ritz-Carlton's hiring process is deliberately stringent.

First up are multistage interviews, which allow the existing executive hotel team to get familiar with the applicant's skills, work personality, responses to theoretical situations, how well the individual's talents fit with the department for which they are applying, and how the individual fits with The Ritz-Carlton's location-specific team.

The detailed interview and selection process allows The Ritz-Carlton to deliver meticulous guest service through employees who have a vested interest in wanting to exceed guests' expectations.

The orientation process after hiring includes a two-day experience that introduces the newly hired associate to the culture by reviewing the company's history, milestones and, most important, service expectations. Throughout the process, employees are taught how to focus on building and fostering relationships with hotel guests. This includes external ones visiting the hotel and internal ones working alongside them.

During orientation, every new employee's preferences are recorded and loaded into The Ritz-Carlton's proprietary Mystique database. Mystique tracks the preferences of guests and employees. The Ritz-Carlton uses this information to ensure that no matter which property a guest or employee is at, they feel at home and comfortable.

Training and development continues long after the initial orientation. Empowerment — taking ownership — is the common denominator among all elements of The Ritz-Carlton's programs.

And empowerment is married to training.

"Do what you do so well that they will want to see it again and bring their friends."
—Walt Disney

Included among the numerous initiatives are the All Aboard class, which focuses on achieving complete guest engagement; updates in safety training; peer-to-peer mentoring; and regular instruction on how to be better-trained observers, able to more effectively read guests' actions and craft on-the-fly ways to deliver The Unexpected over and over again.

Just as important, The Ritz-Carlton recognizes and celebrates team members who deliver The Unexpected.

Employees who go above and beyond to deliver memorable experiences are recognized through The Ritz-Carlton's quarterly Five-Star Awards. From that group, a group of Five-Star Employees of the Year are selected. The organization also publicly shares stories of its team members and the experiences they deliver for guests, keeping The Ritz-Carlton legend alive.

But the same ideas The Ritz-Carlton employs can be applied to nearly any organization — even those that don't necessarily rely on technology and proprietary software. Being detail-oriented and thinking about how to anticipate customers' needs are the key traits needed to deliver that memorable experience. When it comes to restaurants, it's what separates the good ones from the truly great ones.

Some restaurants earn a reputation for amazing food; others for providing stellar service in an upscale environment. Boston-based L'Espalier has earned a reputation for both. And it is due to the meticulous attention to detail paid by chef and owner Frank McClelland to creating an unexpected experience for every restaurant goer that L'Espalier has established itself as one of the nation's must visit establishments.

If it started and ended with McClelland's famous seasonal degustation menus or creative dishes, it would still be enough to draw visitors from all corners of the nation and make even the most fervent foodie add L'Espalier to his or her bucket list. But the reality is that it requires more than simply great food to earn the AAA Five-Diamond Award 14 years in a row, as well as an impressive laundry list of accolades from publications and associations worldwide. So chalk it up to McClelland's unwavering commitment to anticipating customer's needs and delivering The Unexpected as the primary reasons why L'Espalier has catapulted to legendary status.

In interview after interview, McClelland touts the need to deliver amazing culinary creations. But he also says he believes you must go beyond the food to create a memorable experience for diners, and that means injecting The Unexpected into both the culinary and service sides of the equation.

While you might be surprised and delighted by the dishes L'Espalier's staff creates — including empowering his wait staff to deliver samples to customers as they see fit — it's the other intangible parts of the experience that leave even longer lasting impressions.

For example, in January 2013 at the restaurant's monthly afternoon tea tasting, visitors arrived to find a full-fledged Mad Hatter's Tea Party, including a white rabbit at the entrance and a series of rare first editions of Lewis Carroll's "Alice's Adventures in Wonderland." In addition, book-themed items peppered the entire restaurant and enhanced the experience.

These included lingonberry frangipane "Eat Me" cakes and "Drink Me" bottles of iced tea and ginger ale.

Under McClelland's direction, The Unexpected permeates L'Espalier's culture. Employees are empowered to actively seek out opportunities to create new stories for visitors to tell by anticipating their needs, whether it's returning from the restroom to find a fresh, neatly folded napkin in the shape of something new and exciting or finishing dinner only to have a small, hand-wrapped box of freshly baked cookies delivered with the check. Diners tweet experiences of arriving for a regular reservation and being shuttled unknowingly to a private four-person table in the kitchen, where they had the unique pleasure of seeing the gourmet restaurant's legendary kitchen operations in action. And they recount seeing midnight conga lines composed of servers and wait staff beating on pots and pans, entertaining late-night eaters.

McClelland stretches the boundaries of epicurean experiences by empowering his front-line team to think creatively and innovate at every level. After all, for a night out that could end up costing more than $100 per person, you don't really have much leeway to make mistakes. And like The Ritz-Carlton, L'Espalier continues to deliver surprise and delight time after time, making the lofty price tag feel more like the price of entry to an unexpected experience that you'll rave about rather than a high-end bill for a luxury night out.

13 Treat People Like Family

A colleague of my co-author used to take her son to Chick-fil-A once a week as part of their regular weekly "out to dinner" ritual. This began shortly after she and her husband separated, and was a way she was bonding with her son to help the two of them get through the stressful situation.

During one particularly nasty Northeast Ohio winter, in near blizzard-like conditions, the two trekked through the snow to Chick-fil-A so the woman didn't disappoint her son.

They ordered their food — like usual — and then the mother realized she had left her wallet sitting on the counter at her home. Embarrassed, she meekly told the employee at the cash register what had happened and asked if they would hold the food for them while she and her son went home to get money.

The employee said not to worry. She recognized the woman and her son because they came in every Friday night for dinner. She said she would make a note and the next time they came in, they could pay for the meal.

Grateful, and surprised by this unexpected gesture of kindness, the mother thanked the employee, collected the food and sat down with her son to eat.

A few moments later, Daniel Curran, the Chick-fil-A franchisee who owned the Rocky River, Ohio, location, strolled over to their table. He proceeded to inform them that their meal was "on the house."

The mother and her son were so surprised that they nearly cried. As it turned out, the employee at the counter let Curran know what had transpired. And Curran, who prides himself on knowing his customers, recognized the two as regulars. In Curran's eyes, they were more than customers — they were members of his extended family. And in the true family spirit, Curran did not want the woman worrying about not being able to pay today, nor have to remember to pay the following week.

Treating customers like family — and finding ways to ensure you're going above and beyond for them by delivering The Unexpected — can be a magical experience that provides immeasurable satisfaction to both the deliverer and the recipient. In another instance, in July 2014 a widow in Missouri who had celebrated three straight decades of wedding anniversaries with her husband at Red Lobster was the recipient of a truly unexpected experience.

The woman's husband had passed away a few months earlier after an unsuccessful battle with cancer. She and her daughter decided to honor the man's memory and continue the tradition for a 31st year. They went to dinner at a Red Lobster in Columbia, Missouri, and when asked by their server if they were celebrating anything special, the daughter let her know they were there for her mother's 31st anniversary but that her father had recently passed away.

After taking their drink orders, the server approached the manager and asked if they could do anything special for the pair — such as a free dessert or appetizer.

His response: "Let's take care of the meal."

And so, at the end of the meal, in lieu of a bill, the pair found the following note delivered to their table:

"We are sorry to hear about your husband's passing, but we appreciate your loyalty in spending 31 years of your anniversary with us. For

your appreciation your meal is on us! We look forward to spending your next anniversary with us!

Sincerely, Red Lobster + your server, Taylor."

Within a matter of hours, news of the note went viral.

People generally don't expect organizations to treat them like members of their family. But doing so truly defines some of those best organizations that effectively ply The Unexpected.

So what is it that families do differently that these organizations embody?

First, they look out for and help each other when they stumble and fall. They help family members out of tough situations — whether it's comforting them when they're sad or learning how to be empathetic and see the world through each other's eyes. Families teach the life skills necessary to survive and thrive in the world. They make sure other family members are healthy. They send presents when they're least expected. And most important, they simply do those little things that make other family members feel more a part of the family.

Few of these things are typically associated with organizations whose main goal is achieving profitability. But that's where practitioners of The Unexpected differ from the rest. It's an attitude that is ingrained in the corporate culture. It defines who an organization truly is, and can make or break its ability to succeed where other, less attuned competitors, fail. And, for those who get it, the results can be incredible.

At Chick-fil-A, for example, management considers its "treat people like family" culture as the very foundation of its success. The Atlanta-based company generates more than $5 billion in annual revenue at its close to 1,800 locations. Since its founding in 1946 by S. Truett Cathy, finding ways to deliver The Unexpected is something Chick-fil-A has done quite well. Today, that culture is driven by Dan Cathy, the founder's son, whose own commitment is so strong that he encourages any guest to publicly share his or her story online at www.chick-fil-a.com/Story.

Appropriately, the description on the site reads:

"Every now and then Chick-fil-A customers have an experience so unexpected, so wonderful, they just have to share it. Read some of these stories here and submit your own!"

Starting The Unexpected

Step 1 of 3:

- Establish a servant culture

So how do Chick-fil-A franchisees and employees work in unison to fulfill the same mission?

They start early, investing significant time identifying, vetting and granting franchisee licenses to the right people from among the more than 20,000 applications received each year. The process is extremely stringent, and only those who demonstrate the right stuff are selected.

On a more granular level, the process continues by hiring attentive and courteous team members who are extensively trained to keep the customer first and identify opportunities to create surprise and delight through Chick-fil-A's Team Member Development Process.

Step One is called Visions and Values. Chick-fil-A's philosophy is that unless every new team member has an understanding of what Chick-fil-A, as an organization, believes is important, subsequent training is a waste.

The Cathy family doesn't want Chick-fil-A to be merely good. They want to be great. In fact, one of Truett's more famous mottos was "Perfection is expected, excellence will be accepted."

In keeping with its commitment to continuous improvement — another trait families instill in each other — Chick-fil-A's orientation handbook remains with the new team member throughout his or her first few weeks. Among the ways it is used is as an explanation of each day — what it will look like, what will be expected of the new team member — and how the new employee's role fits into the greater service-oriented goals of the organization.

Next, a more experienced team member is designated as the Unit Training Coordinator (UTC) — a sort of "big brother," if you will. The UTC partners with the new team member to answer questions, walk them through orientation, help integrate them into the local team, and teach them how to identify opportunities to go above and beyond with customers at every point of contact.

And then, once they're in the field, nearly all Chick-fil-A franchise owners have developed some sort of recognition program to reward employees that deliver unexpected service. "I sometimes hold contests among our team members to keep track of how many people they can make smile," Curran says.

At Curran's location, he goes one step further, aiming to provide an even greater level of unexpected family-oriented opportunities for his best customers.

"Ultimately, we don't just want to create fans of Chick-fil-A," he says. "We want to create Raving Fans — someone who comes often and tells others about us. Raving Fans also recognize the quality and value of our product, which negates the need to compete on price."

On one occasion, Curran and his team even sent written invitations to 30 of their best Raving Fans for a special dinner.

Upon arrival, the people were greeted at the door and escorted to their reserved seats. "We served them a free three-course dinner in their honor, complete with linen table cloths, silverware, table-side service, roses and parting gifts for each guest," Curran says.

And, of course, before, during and after the event, Curran's customers couldn't believe what was happening.

"It was pretty amazing," he says. "The response was just incredible — these customers felt as if we had made them members of our family and held a massive family dinner."

There are thousands of stories just like this collected online at Chick-fil-A's corporate website, where they are shared publicly and internally among the Chick-fil-A faithful — including franchise owners and their employees.

Explains Cathy: "We are blessed with a family of operators and team members whose daily commitment to excellence and heartfelt, personalized service creates an atmosphere of hospitality that is unparalleled in our industry. The Chick-fil-A brand will remain vibrant as long as we remain focused on providing an experience that our guests love to brag about."

Starting The Unexpected

Step 2 of 3:

- Empower frontline people to identify opportunities to make creative and innovative decisions on how to deliver service to clients.

The results of Chick-fil-A's efforts are just as impressive as the actions themselves. The company has nearly 3,000 fewer locations than its closest rival KFC, yet it generates nearly $1 billion more in annual revenue — equating to a whopping $3 million in annual sales per Chick-fil-A location. That's an impressive figure for individual fast food restaurants, but one even more impressive when you consider that Chick-fil-A is closed on Sundays.

Yes, that's right. Chick-fil-A operates only six days per week. Part of its family-first culture is that Chick-fil-A encourages its franchisees, employees — and even customers — to spend Sundays with their own families and loved ones.

Another trait families demonstrate is the ability to empathize — learning how to see life through that person's eyes. So what better way for a company to get to know its customers better than to have employees walk in their shoes? It's something you'd rarely, if ever, expect from a company, much less a multibillion-dollar manufacturer that doesn't sell directly to its end user.

Traditionally, manufacturers try to build one of two cultures — that of efficient factory, where products are churned out on time, on budget and with as few defects as possible; or that of innovation factory, where the culture and how team members deliver service to clients is just as, if not more, important.

Those that opt for the latter have the ability to deliver The Unexpected much more often. And, when your product is medical equipment — specifically wheelchairs — getting to know your end customer as intimately as if they were members of your own family can add an entirely new layer of being able to deliver unexpected experiences.

At Invacare Corporation, a global medical equipment manufacturer that's best known for its primary product, wheelchairs, being able to effectively marry innovation with treating customers like family has been a critical part of the company's success.

Invacare's name quite literally means "Innovation in health care," and its leadership team recognizes that a focus on service is the perfect complement to its innovative and high quality products.

"During our new [customer service representative] hire training, the class is introduced to our departmental mantra, or service policy of 'Exceptional Service, Every Time, Through Employee Empowerment,'" explains Elizabeth Gwynn, Invacare's former customer service director. "Early introduction to this philosophy lays the foundation for great service and provides the team with the awareness and support to be self-directed and to have confidence in their own abilities to do what is right on behalf of the customer and our organization."

Invacare's intensive customer service representative training program lasts five weeks, and includes modules on products, phone skills and how to listen to what customers are really saying.

Taking ownership of each call answered is an important part of the company's empowerment culture, which encourages them to "kick it up a notch" and provide above and beyond world-class customer service. Accordingly, customer service representatives regularly take it upon themselves to be the ones to develop solutions for clients who call into the service center — even if it would have been easier to redirect the customers to other experts.

But that's not how Invacare team members truly understand their customers — and how it has been able to best ply The Unexpected. That comes from the company's A Day in a Chair program, which every customer service representative participates in shortly after they complete their initial training.

Starting The Unexpected

Step 3 of 3:

- Formalize systems within your company that allow for The Unexpected to occur.

During "A Day in a Chair," team members spend one full day in one of Invacare's wheelchairs, going about their daily tasks with the same limitations each of Invacare's end customers must deal with. The program provides team members with the opportunity to experience firsthand the daily challenges of wheelchair users.

As Gwynn explains, "(It) enhances the customer service representative's ability to empathize with consumers and promotes the realization that a wheelchair is more than just a product; it is critical to the quality of life for someone."

Again, that's what families do — learn how to empathize so that they can help improve the quality of life of those who are part of it.

Enter San Francisco-based Hint Inc., where founder and CEO Kara Goldin instills a belief in her team that every day, each individual has the opportunity to make a difference in someone's life — whether big or small. It is, says Goldin, what you do for people you care about.

Living a healthy life is at the core of Hint; and education is an important part of how Hint's team members spread the word — often in surprising ways. Think of it Goldin like a mother or your older sister who is constantly looking out for other family members' health and spreading the gospel about ways to be healthier.

One way Hint is spreading the word is by engaging its fans to share their own healthy life ideas with others. And with more than 225,000 likes on Facebook, the company has a lot of people who participate in the family functions.

But while other companies invite their audience to share feedback or stories by posting to the Facebook page alone, Goldin adds her own element of surprise and delight by going one step further — she invites people to become regular guest bloggers on Hint's main website.

People can apply to blog in four different categories:

- Healthy life hints, which include topics like nutrition, fitness, stress relief, mindful living and healthy relationships.
- Simple life hints, which include topics such as two-to-five ingredient recipes, DIY projects, drink recipes and how-to posts.
- Upgraded life hints, which include topics such as how to upgrade your life.
- Entrepreneurial life hints, which may include interviews with cool business-minded folk, career success tips, and inspiration and how-to advice on following your dreams.

This level of engagement has helped Goldin build a new type of community and strengthen her company's brand. And she's always seeking new ways to build champions committed to improving people's health.

"We encourage our employees to be liberal with offering samples and bottles of Hint and Hint Fizz," says Goldin, who is also an EY Entrepreneurial Winning Women™ 2012 Awards honoree. "The best way to engage a potential customer is to give them an opportunity to try your product."

This concept isn't new. Grocery stores do it all the time. But Goldin and her team break ranks with conventional wisdom of offering samples. Their passion to deliver The Unexpected to people who have never tried Hint Water is contagious, and Goldin's husband, Theo, the company's COO, leads it.

"Theo never goes anywhere without several bottles of Hint on him," Goldin explains. "If he meets someone who has never tried Hint, he gives him or her a bottle — no matter where he encounters them."

Imagine that: You're out and about with your family in the park on a sunny Sunday afternoon. A friendly stranger approaches with an unexpected surprise — bottles of Hint Water for everyone. Where else other than within a family could something like that happen?

With such a focus on extending its family by delivering surprise and delight, it should come as little surprise that Hint has been on a sustained upward curve of success. Musician John Legend was so enamored that he joined the Hint family and invested in the company. And in 2013, revenue grew by more than 40 percent as Hint was selected as one of 14 beverages to be part of the national Drink Up campaign launched by the White House, an initiative that encourages people to make healthier drink choices.

One of the most basic lessons families teach are the general life skills necessary to survive in society. For the most part, they're straightforward — wake up in the morning, dress professionally, be responsible, make an honest living. Rarely are those things unexpected. But when those basic lessons are taught by a for-profit company as part of its core mission, that's truly The Unexpected in action.

New York-based LearnVest is one of those organizations. Alexa von Tobel, founder and CEO, believes that smart financial knowledge must be taught in much the same way a parent "teaches a child to fish" once they're old enough to learn how to feed themselves. Being self-sufficient in life is critical and as unexpected as it seems an organization to put that component first and foremost as its mission, von Tobel's vision has helped her build a new kind of company and establish a name for herself as one of the new breed of socially conscious entrepreneurs.

A 2011 Harvard graduate, von Tobel founded LearnVest with the goal of becoming the leading online site for women who wanted to learn how to better manage their money. It's something she noticed that not enough families instilled in the daughters.

She started offering free educational content, a variety of financial calculators, and daily newsletters that help teach women how to earn well, save well and spend well. Soon thereafter, von Tobel complemented this with a series of paid services to provide access to financial managers and more personalized advice and information.

But as the company grew, von Tobel recognized that her customers were really becoming members of her extended family, and she started thinking about what she would do if they were her children who needed this type of advice.

> "We see our customers as invited guests to a party, and we are the hosts. It's our job every day to make every important aspect of the customer experience a little bit better."
> —Jeff Bezos, CEO, Amazon

So she did something completed unexpected — she reached out and solicited input from the site's burgeoning number of users to help transform her organization.

Von Tobel understood that LearnVest could be a much more effective tool if it engaged its members to tell her what they thought they needed to know in order to effectively learn how to fish. She could have simply started trying out new ideas and implementing the ones she liked best one at a time. Instead, she formed LearnVest Labs, which today delivers The Unexpected to customers in ways they have never experienced from other financial education organizations.

In a move usually reserved for technology companies in the most innovative Silicon Valley organizations, von Tobel established rigorous product creation processes for building and testing new potential LearnVest products and services. Chief among these processes was bringing in live users to evaluate the opportunities.

"It came from listening," von Tobel says. As of year-end 2013, there were more than 7,500 vetted users testing products and services to evaluate which are most viable to help users "learn how to fish."

The final test is an actual sniff test that asks, "Is this something that I would use every day to make my financial life better?"

"If new products don't pass all of those tests, they don't come to market," she says.

And why should they? You don't take chances with your family...even if you want to deliver surprise and delight.

Finally, close-knit families surprise other family members with gifts at other times throughout the year besides birthdays and holidays — most often when they least expect it. Georgia-based asset-management investment firm Balentine thinks about how it delivers The Unexpected in much the same way.

Balentine out hustles larger-manned competitors by delivering memorable moments to clients that cements the Balentine name firmly in their minds. By doing so, they've come to think about every client like a member of each employee's respective family.

Under the direction of Brittain Prigge, a founding partner and director of client relationships, Balentine employees personalize the experience. "We let them understand that we know what's going on in their lives and we care," Prigge says.

Prigge and her team do more than just work diligently to protect and grow their clients' assets — that's what is expected. And it wasn't until Prigge challenged her client relationship management team to up the ante on service that things really began to click.

"I said, 'OK, every week I'm going to point to somebody and you're going to have to come up with an idea for a client,'" she recalls. "'It can't have anything to do with investments, and it has to be something that relates to something you learned about them on a one-on-one basis or that was mentioned during a meeting. And it should be something that might be beneficial just for them. You have to make a difference.'"

Prigge's challenge sparked intense competition among the company's 20-something employees, along with constant chatter about how they might learn to pay better attention to their clients so that they, too, could identify an opportunity to deliver something truly unexpected.

"I said, 'Take ownership. See your opportunities and do something about it.' And we set aside a small budget to pay for it," Prigge says. "And so for one client, my colleague pitched me with three great ideas that we went with. Together, they cost about $428 to do for a client that represented $75 million worth of client assets. And then everyone began to look at this and ask, 'How could we not be doing this all along?'"

The firm's ideas have not been complicated, but they've been highly effective. Among the ones that have made a difference:

- Sending a meal to a client receiving out of state medical care.
- Giving a college care package to a client entering her freshman year of college.
- Mailing a book mentioned during a meeting.
- Taking a client to a birthday luncheon.
- Sending "Georgia-themed" goodie baskets to new, out-of-state clients.
- Donating to clients' favorite charities as holiday gifts.

"None of us are content," Prigge says. "We push each other. We have an exceptional group of people with a lot of type A's pushing each other to do better and better. I think that's The Unexpected above-and-beyond we provide. This is all about our clients. They're family."

14 Going The Second Mile

At the height of the Roman Empire's power, its soldiers would demonstrate their superiority over conquered nations by forcing the conquered people to carry their equipment — at a distance up to one mile. Accordingly, people would make the one-mile journey as slaves.

Over time, however, a few people started to challenge the soldiers — but not by refusing to carry their equipment. Instead, they offered to carry it for two miles instead of one. In essence, their statement was both subtle and profound: You cannot enslave those who possess free will and choose to serve. Or, as stated in Matthew 5:41, "And whosoever shall compel thee to go one mile, go with him two."

Today, the concept of "going the extra mile" has become a common term, but few recognize its more historical significance.

Everyone deserves first-mile service. But truly exceptional organizations — those that effectively deliver The Unexpected — find myriad ways to surprise and delight their customers with second mile service.

They understand that it starts — and ends — with front-line team members. They make it a priority to invest in, mentor and empower people to have free license to be creative with how they deliver second-mile service.

At Deck Rescue LLC, a Litchfield, Ohio-based exterior wood restoration company that specializes in decks and fences, president and founder David Hydock recognizes that second mile service is his only competitive advantage. Deck Rescue operates in a crowded, on-location home improvement space. Because of that, Hydock faces significant operational challenges, not the least of which is overcoming skepticism from prospective clients because the deck restoration sector has been long known for its less-than-reputable contractors.

"You see the news segments every year about folks who have been bilked out of their money or received less of a service than what they paid for," Hydock explains. "We have never sold a job on price, making the emphasis instead on outstanding customer service."

So not only does Deck Rescue give clients what they pay for — deck cleaning, restoration services and stain work — but Hydock encourages his employees to deliver something more.

"On every job, we seek out an additional free service to provide," Hydock says. "It may be something tiny — such as washing down their siding, patio furniture or brick patio — but we find something free to provide. It may even be unrelated to the deck restoration, such as bringing their newspaper or trash cans to their house from the curb. It's amazing what you can find when you are looking for it."

With 10 franchised locations across three states — South Carolina, Indiana and Ohio — Hydock faces additional challenges, such as not having the luxury to operate year-round. In the northern areas where his organization has locations, Deck Rescue operates only from April to November.

Hydock effectively manages those seasonal business limitations by building market share and establishing a loyal client base by placing a heavy emphasis on teaching franchise owners and employees how to recognize opportunities to go that second mile when clients least expect it.

One such way is rewarding loyal clients who work with Deck Rescue on a frequent basis — such as establishing a regular cleaning schedule and sticking to it. Those people become part of the company's Loyalty Rewards Program and never experience a price increase. "The company sends postcard reminders in the spring to remind them of the reward program — and the fact that there is no price increase," he says. "We often hear from them a few days after that, saying how surprised they are."

Like other organizations that best deliver The Unexpected, Hydock publicly acknowledges employees who do it well. He regularly reiterates to every employee and franchise owner why delivering unexpected customer service is so important to Deck Rescue's success — and then highlights the best examples each year at the annual meeting of franchise owners.

"We go around the room and give examples of how we provided exemplary customer service," Hydock says. "I also have a questionnaire on their monthly loyalty form, asking them to tell me what additional service they provided their clients — at no additional charge."

But Hydock takes that one step further — Deck Rescue does not pay its employees on an hourly basis. Instead, it has developed a pay structure based on proficiency and client satisfaction. Employees are paid a percentage of the price charged to homeowners.

The percentage method of pay provides employees a reason to make the homeowner happy by identifying ways to surprise them and etch the company's reputation for delivering The Unexpected in their collective memories, Hydock says.

Employees are further incentivized two additional ways: Those with no callbacks (incomplete jobs that need to be redone) or complaints throughout the month are given an additional month-end bonus. And, if homeowners go out of their way to compliment a Deck Rescue employee, another bonus is paid out.

To Hydock, tying compensation to service makes good business sense. And, he doesn't understand why more organizations don't do the same.

"Hourly pay breeds lackadaisical and sloth-like behavior from employees," Hydock says. "If they are paid hourly, what is their incentive to excel? Why go above and beyond when your employer doesn't care."

But not all organizations have the organizational structure necessary to pay employees a percentage of each customer transaction. In larger organizations, however, where there are so many customers and transactions involved, public recognition can have the same power.

Such is the case at Cox Communications, the third-largest cable entertainment and broadband services provider in the nation, where delivering second mile service happens because the company hires the right people and has established formal programs to regularly acknowledge employees' above-and-beyond efforts.

Among them, Cox provides an open forum for employees to talk about the joy they receive delivering The Unexpected, and it shares those second mile success stories across the entire organization.

One example is Cox's New England-Cleveland Region's Moments of Trust program, which recognizes employees who show they are committed to acting as a trusted provider to customers. Leaders are encouraged to nominate employees who have gone the extra mile, and at the end of each year, one employee is selected as that year's Moments of Trust winner.

When your tag line is "Your Friend in the Digital Age," you're setting a pretty high bar for delivering customer service — especially when you have 6.5 million customers spread across the nation. But just delivering what customers want and need isn't enough for Cox. It is constantly looking for ways to take its consumer service offerings to a higher level. And Cox is one of those rare organizations that possess both the resources and the willpower to accomplish the job.

Training is a critical part of the equation — new employees are taught through examples that Cox stands behind its claim to provide the best customer service in the industry, as well as how to identify opportunities to create a "wow" experience.

And Cox maintains this philosophy at the highest levels of the organizations. After all, you can't expect employees to follow what they consider as lip service. You might lead by example. So Cox begins by asking team members to do something basic, yet filled with common sense — they ask the customer what they want and then intently listen to the subtext.

Feedback for crafting ways to surprise the customer with something they're not expecting is gathered through quarterly customer satisfaction surveys, live conversations with customers, after-service reports and collecting feedback from client interactions at every level.

Based on the information collected — some direct, some inferred, some interpreted — Cox analyzes it and builds systems to improve its service. But it also looks for those little things customers are saying.

To achieve this, Cox developed its Voice of the Customer Surveys (VOC). Early on, Cox's VOCs revealed customers wanted to have a relationship with a trusted partner. So the company developed a systematic customer listening engine that combines technology with the human information-gathering element. Working in tandem, these tools have helped Cox evolve its ideas to deliver The Unexpected.

One such example is how Cox conducts in-home service calls.

More than 15 years ago, Cox service representatives who scheduled in-home technician service calls for customers noticed an increasing frustration among clients because of the absence of specific service appointment arrival times. At the time, it was common practice in the telecommunications industry — as well as other industries — to ask customers to set aside a half-day or full day to wait for a service technician to arrive at their homes.

Seeing an opportunity to "wow" its customer by delivering something completely unexpected, Cox rolled out a two-hour appointment window and backed it up with an on-time guarantee. If the Cox service technician failed to arrive during the announced two-hour window, the customer was credited $20 to his or her account.

After being floored by the move, savvy competitors quickly followed suit, and today, specific time windows — and penalties — are industry standard.

And then, an amazing confluence of factors happened at Cox. First, technicians, arriving to find customers delighted by the specific time window, heard consumers talk about how wonderful it would be if they could have this great two-hour time window on the same day they called to make an appointment. At the same time, customer service satisfaction surveys (part of Cox's listening engine) began reflecting the same notion. Thus was born Cox's same-day service calls — another industry breakthrough.

By identifying opportunities to deliver unexpected second mile service to its clients, Cox continued its evolution — and its growth.

A few years ago, Cox extended its service hours to include all-day Saturday. And then, it extended service calls to Sunday. Both moves generated significant buzz — both online through social media and through traditional media channels.

> "Always do more than is required of you."
> —Gen. George S. Patton

Today, more than 95 percent of Cox's service calls are handled within 24 hours of the customers' preferred time frame, and more than 50 percent of Cox's service business is conducted on nights and weekends.

Another example of how Cox employees are empowered to identify opportunities to deliver The Unexpected is how they show respect for customers' homes.

Several years ago, technicians noticed that during inclement weather they sometimes tracked dirt into customer's homes and needed to clean it up before they left. Cox service center members noticed the same thing after analyzing its VOC feedback. So the company implemented a new program where technicians spent a few extra minutes putting protective booties over their shoes to ensure they didn't track mud, dirt or rain into a customer's home.

In 2013, employees took that initiative one step further — they began bringing small hand-held vacuum cleaners with them so they could clean up after the service call was complete.

Another organization that constantly seeks ways to deliver second mile service is Case-Mate, which designs and sells mobile accessory cases for smartphones and tablets. The company partners with celebrities, musicians and artists to allow consumers to literally design their own case online and then buy it.

Case-Mate founder and CEO Shashi Reddy recognizes that when it comes to his organization's ability to create personal connections with prospects and existing clients — and deliver an experience that goes beyond expectations, the only way to do so is by getting his products in their hands.

Reddy has been known to surprise people who have commented on his cases while standing in line at a coffee shop or at the airport. He's taken the case off one of his personal devices, handed it to the person who commented on it, and said, "I hope you enjoy it." His belief is happiness is truly contagious and he says he's in the business of spreading it.

When your tag line and business philosophy says "Happiness by design," you better find ways to deliver happiness wherever you can. And, as creating surprise and delight are key elements of delivering The Unexpected, it's often the little things that make something "personalized" rise to the level of legendary.

Case-Mate's Customer Experience Group employs state-of-the-art e-commerce platforms that track customers' purchases, log consumer interactions and identify trends. That technology combines with formal training for all new hires, as well as continuous informal training for existing hires.

Formal training takes two weeks, and is followed by a 90-day initiation period where each staff member is evaluated for their ability to respond to customers and prospects in such as a way where the end-result makes happiness happen.

During the formal training, staff members are taught the usual information — about the products and systems in place — but they're also instructed on the importance of identifying opportunities to deliver a higher level of happiness.

To that end, Case-Mate's Customer Experience Group engages with people online and offline, identifying those opportunities where a little extra effort leads to the end result — happiness. And Reddy encourages them to do so.

For example, they may send extra items as a "thank you" or "just because" in order to surprise customers. They may engage with a customer or prospect online about a case, and then send a sample in the mail for them to try. Case-Mate's team creates contests, develops new product ideas in conjunction with feedback, and finds ways to get people talking.

Those consumers subsequently share those experiences online through social media. Case-Mate has built a loyal following of people who can't wait to see what's next. Nearly 700,000 people like Case-Mate on Facebook, and those little extras have 10,000-plus people regularly buzzing about the products and the service they receive.

With social media so ubiquitous in today's society, finding ways to implement technology as a tool to deliver The Unexpected is becoming that much more important.

At Greensboro, North Carolina-based Kotis Properties, which owns Darryl's Wood Fired Grill, president and CEO Marty Kotis has achieved both regional and national attention for Darryl's use of social media — particularly for its employees' use of Twitter to engage with customers.

"We're involved with many of the social mediums out there — Twitter, Facebook, Foursquare, Yelp and others," Kotis says. "And we're connecting and responding rapidly to our guests' concerns and suggestions — then taking action based on it. We may have a person in the restaurant that tweets about Darryl's, which is one of our properties, and we reply back while they're in the restaurant. Nobody is expecting that to happen. It's one thing to surprise them by providing a personalized response. It's another to do so while they're still an active guest. That's completely unexpected."

Kotis says people tweet that they're in the restaurant and having a good time. "We might respond back by asking, 'How is everything?'" he says. "If they say something like, 'Good, but the music's a little loud,' we let the manager know and the manager might instantly adjust the music level in that specific section of the restaurant. People are blown away."

The same type of unexpected service occurs when someone tweets a not-so-positive experience.

"We engage with them immediately via social media," Kotis says. "And then we send someone over to address the issue. Nobody expects that from a restaurant."

Kotis readily admits he adapted the practice of customer engagement via social media by looking at how other consumer-related organizations did it. His version became so successful that he expanded from doing it himself to teaching other team members how they could use social media to find ways to do things completely unexpected for customers.

It appears to be working. As of February 2014, nearly 70,000 people liked Darryl's on Facebook and more than 4,000 people followed it on Twitter. Both are significant numbers when you take into account the fact that Darryl's has only one location.

"I had a Twitter exchange with someone who was thinking about coming into the restaurant," Kotis recalls, referring to an incident that garnered national attention. "He was planning a birthday dinner and considering Darryl's as an option. Through Twitter, we sold him on coming in and giving us a try."

Once there, the gentlemen tweeted with the restaurant (@darryls) throughout his meal. It was an engaging, entertaining conversation. And it earned Darryl's more business from the guest — he booked an upcoming 50-person event.

"You talk about delivering The Unexpected," Kotis says. "This was it in action. We were able to provide the guest with a memorable experience he would not have been able to get anywhere else. Because of that, he told everyone he knew — he even tweeted it out to everyone who followed him — and that really created new customers for us. And with that gentleman it absolutely created a customer for life."

Today, Kotis has identified yet another opportunity to deliver that unexpected second mile service — he has replaced the traditional restaurant comment card with the tweet. Explains Kotis, "It's immediate, and creates a wow factor that others just don't deliver. When we did that, nobody saw it coming."

Delivering The Unexpected when nobody sees it coming is the true definition of second mile service.

"Sadly, it seems as though expectations of customer service have reached such low levels throughout much of business that creating The Unexpected has become somewhat easier," says Patty Klein, CEO of South Florida-based A-Plus Meetings & Incentives, a corporate conference management and incentive tips company. "We find that most of the time, creating it comes from the simple things: Really listening to our customers and acting on what they are asking for in ways that go above and beyond."

For example, one of the attendees at a conference A-Plus was running a few years ago approached a member of Klein's team with a broken watch.

"He was from Chile, and asked our staff member at the hospitality desk if we knew where he might be able to get it fixed quickly as he was flying out the next day," Klein recalls. "An expected response might have been to search for a watch repair shop nearby and give him the contact information."

However, the team member's response was to take the watch and tell him they would handle it, so he could get back into the meetings.

"Our associate found the best place, drove the watch there, waited for it to be fixed and paid the bill," Klein says. "Within two hours, we had the watch back in his hands."

The guest was so amazed that he went to the CEO of his company and let him know about it.

"From a simple request we ended up with a life-long, happy attendee and a CEO who knew about the level of unexpected service we provide to every single attendee at the events we manage," Klein says. "By listening to our customers and empowering our employees to go the extra step, we're able to provide unexpected service."

When you take that extra step and carry the equipment a second mile, the good will you engender can have meaning far beyond a vendor-client relationship.

"One of our client teams was working around the clock to produce launch materials for a client that had two significant drug launches to execute within 60 days," says Lisa Bair, CEO of Hobart Group Holdings, a New Jersey-based company that delivers strategic, account, medical and creative services — including database and market research, advertising and promotion, sales training, and contract and price management to its clients. "The teams were working to get all of the materials updated per the client requests, and then get them approved for use in the field.

"One of the things we had launched internally as a branded freebie for the staff was a series of Hobart energy drinks to keep energy high, even during long and late hours," says Bair, an EY Entrepreneurial Winning Women™ 2010 Awards honoree. "So our agency team had the idea to ship several cases of the drinks to the extended client team they were working with so that everyone on the case had the energy to keep working on getting all the materials finished and approved."

Needless to say, when the cases arrived, the client was surprised. "They were ecstatic," says Bair. "Here was a team who was working on just a few hours of sleep, and they had gone out of their way to keep everyone's spirits high during the most critical period of the work. We later heard that the clients not only consumed the drinks but began an internal game of cat-and-mouse, swiping and hoarding each other's supply. After the launch, this client sent a great email to thank the team for their tireless efforts and made a point to note how surprised they were by receiving the energy drinks, and how great they were in helping them make it through to the launch. It was a true customer 'Wow!'"

Finally, delivering second mile service can be something as simple as taking that extra step to enhance your organization's relationship with partners in your supply chain — delivering The Unexpected long before your product or service ever reaches it end user.

"We send surprise gifts to reps or those we interact with and wish to leave a lasting impression on," explains Kari Warberg Block, founder & CEO of Earth-Kind, the manufacturer and distributor of the only Environmental Protection Agency-certified natural rodent repellent, Fresh Cab Block. "The only rule is that the gifts can't be expected or ordinary. It must make the recipient feel a moment of delight ... and it must be handmade. Most important, we never repeat the same gift twice."

Some gifts have been handcrafted chocolate mice, home-baked carrot cake, baskets of fresh flowers and other specialties. "If possible, we try to deliver the gift in person, by an employee who wouldn't normally interact with the recipient," Block says.

Block also uses the company's website (www.earth-kind.com) and blog to highlight vendors who aren't expecting any sort of reciprocation for carrying Fresh Cab. "I look for ways to share their own stories, passions and values," she says.

"Straight from the Top," Block's blog, has highlighted such items as True Value's foundation and the good work the charitable arm of the hardware chain does in communities nationwide. She has also featured Tractor Supply Co., a 70-year-old business that has grown from a mail-order catalog business to a chain of more than 1,150 stores nationwide.

Block saw a news item on TV one night about TSC, which had partnered with Earth-Kind since 2008 and carried Fresh Cab. So she decided to share the story she saw on her blog:

"Seeing their success in times like these reaffirms my belief that success in business can happen when everyone is looking out for the best interest of the customer, regardless of what everyone else is doing," Block wrote. "Kudos to the CEO, Jim Wright, for doubling sales this year without sacrificing quality, service, or vendor relations!"

Then she shared facts about the company and explained what impressed her the most:

"They treat their vendors like partners. You've all heard the horrible stories of that big-box retailer that does everything based on price. When we do business with TSC, it's all based on better serving their customers. Partnering with vendors benefits customers in a couple of ways. TSC doesn't force their vendors to spend tons of money each year going to mandatory trade shows. This saves money on all ends, which is passed on to customers. TSC works directly with a manufacturer to get the best pricing, rather than taking a shortcut and only working with rep agencies carrying hundreds of products. Maintaining this type of direct relationship guarantees customers a high level of expertise, service and superior pricing — a magic mix that can never go wrong."

> On average, loyal customers are worth up to 10 times as much as their first purchase.
> Source: White House Office of Consumer Affairs

Finally, Block shared a link to the company's website. Highlighting your vendors without them asking for it is truly unexpected. And when you think about carrying equipment for a second mile, promoting the Roman Empire without being asked to do so, is something that would have impressed both the Roman soldiers and the emperor, himself.

15 Create One Special Moment That Will Never Be Forgotten

Part of the goal of delivering The Unexpected is creating memorable experiences. More often than not, these happen because an organization trains its employees to identify opportunities to deliver them, and then empowers them to take action. Sometimes, however, delivery of The Unexpected can be a planned event — something designed to create that one special moment that will never be forgotten.

In 2013, one of those moments was delivered by an organization in perhaps the most unlikely of industries — transportation. While airlines worldwide have realized that they can't survive by trying to compete on low-price fares, the shift toward a greater emphasis on service isn't easy. Travelers are picky and often just want to make it from point A to point B with the least amount of hassle. They don't want to pay for extras, yet want a good experience.

> The customer reaction tells you if The Unexpected worked

So what Canadian airline WestJet was able to accomplish during the 2013 holiday season may just go down in history as the greatest example to date in the aviation industry of delivering The Unexpected.

WestJet is the 800-pound gorilla in Canada, employing more than 9,000 people and offering scheduled airline service to 87 destinations in

North America, Central America and the Caribbean. It pioneered low-cost flying in Canada, and prides itself on a culture of caring.

In early December 2013, WestJet pulled off an unexpected Christmas miracle for its clients — and it filmed the entire experience.

"We wanted to turn our holiday campaign into a tradition by doing something that's never been done before," explains WestJet spokesperson Richard Bartrem.

At Toronto Pearson International Airport and John C. Munro Hamilton International Airport, employees set up giant "present" video screens in the respective departure lounges for passengers flying from Toronto and Hamilton to Calgary.

Employees dressed as elves helped escort people to the screens, where they were personally welcomed by a virtual Santa who greeted them each by name and who asked what they wanted for Christmas.

Passengers were amused by the appearance of Santa. They mentioned items such as new socks and underwear, a warm scarf and the traditional assortment of holiday toys. A few people aimed high, going so far as to mention an Android tablet and even a big screen TV.

As Santa listened and chatted with the passengers, real magic was happening behind the scenes. WestJetters, as the airlines' employees are known, were busy taking notes, building a real shopping list.

Once the two Calgary-bound flights took to the air, an army of 150 volunteer WestJetters rushed off to Calgary's malls. They bought toys and dolls, sporting goods, electronics, a big screen TV and many other presents.

Then, their cars filled with gifts, they headed to Calgary International Airport.

Once there, they met fellow employees clad in Santa hats, and together feverishly wrapped hundreds of presents and labeled them with each passenger or family's name. The gift tags were signed, "From Santa."

When the two planes arrived, passengers were shuttled by WestJetters to a carousel to retrieve their luggage.

The baggage claim area was decorated in festive Christmas decorations and WestJetters were out in full force to greet and welcome the travelers.

When the conveyer belts started, the passengers' luggage didn't appear. Instead, a parade of wrapped and tagged presents began coming down the belt filling the luggage carousels.

At first, travelers were confused. But then, the children saw the presents and began tugging at their parents' legs and pointing. The adults moved closer and noticed that the presents had their names on them.

Just as they were began to understand something unexpected and special was going on, Santa appeared in the carousel area. He captured everyone's attention by waving and wishing everyone a Merry Christmas.

Slowly, people started picking up and opening the presents. They weren't sure what to expect. But when they found the very things they had told Santa they wanted, murmurs of surprise and delight spread across the carousel lounge.

> "The way to a customer's heart is much more than a loyalty program. Making customer evangelists is about creating experiences worth talking about."
> —Valeria Maltoni, founder, Conversation Agent; VP of Digital Strategy, PM Digital

There were snowboards, toys, warm scarfs, cameras, Android tablets, and yes, even socks and underwear.

And then everyone stopped to watch as an oversized package was manually loaded onto the carousel and was then presented to the family who had asked for a big screen TV. When they realized what was inside, everyone broke into mass cheering and applause.

It didn't take long for people to begin sharing their unexpected experience with others via social media — instantly creating a legend for WestJet. A few days later, when the video was uploaded to WestJet's YouTube channel, it went viral — more than 3 million people watched it in the first few days. By the end of January 2014, that number snowballed to more than 35 million views.

WestJet's idea for the initiative — filmed and transformed into a holiday video — was actually born over the summer of 2013.

Greg Plata, WestJet's Team Lead of Sponsorship, explains on the company's blog: "In early August, we sat down with our friends at Studio M and started brainstorming what 'giving' looked like at its best. We wanted to do something big, exciting and fresh."

The "big" initiative required 175 WestJet volunteers, as well as coordination among three airports and an appearance from Santa, himself. But it was well worth the effort.

"We made a Christmas miracle happen for more than 250 guests on two Calgary-bound flights," says Plata. "It was about creating a remarkable experience, something that would live with our guests far beyond their WestJet flight."

By delivering The Unexpected to those 250 passengers, WestJet did just that. It not only cemented its position as a company that provides surprise and delight to its customers, it also strengthened its culture of employee caring. Even more impressive, beyond the 35 million video views, WestJet's initiative garnered global media attention. And overnight it became the 2013-2014 winter social media darling.

"This was inspired by the notion of real-time giving," says Bartrem. "We wanted to surprise our guests with meaningful, personalized gifts when they least expected them. Being able to show our guests how much we care with gift-giving, a tried and true holiday tradition, resonates with WestJetters as much as our guests."

Now the only question among WestJet travelers is "What's next?"

16 Make It Fun

Back in the 1970s and early 1980s, there were dozens of regionally based restaurants and ice cream parlors where the staff sang and danced and otherwise made loud noises to entertain their guests — all of which was designed to create an atmosphere of fun.

Around the mid 1980s and early 1990s, however, consumers' desires for restaurant chains changed. The trend toward large national chains that offered cookie-cutter menus grew, putting a heavier emphasis on happy hour for business people and less emphasis on making the experience one of family-friendly fun.

There are, of course, a few exceptions. Dallas-based Chuck E. Cheese's continues its family-friendly "fun" experience — building around loud, colorful video games and small, indoor rides. And chains like The Barnyard and Dave and Buster's have effectively combined the "happy hour" experience with interactive video games for both kids and adults. None of these chains, however, provide the same type of delivery of The Unexpected that the chains of the '70s and '80s were able to do.

Despite this, the idea of creating a fun experience — with a touch of The Unexpected thrown in — has gradually crept back into society. And interestingly, it's coming from some of the unlikeliest of sources.

Consider two world-renowned companies, Volkswagen and Coca-Cola, that are proving when you make something fun — or bring a little happiness into consumers' lives — you can change the perception about your brand.

The idea of making it fun — while not specifically designed to sell a product or serve — will create an unexpected experience and etch a company's brand in consumers' minds. By doing so, consumers will effectively think more positively about the brand. And that, in turn, often results in increased sales.

In 2009, Volkswagen developed an advertising and marketing campaign designed to generate interest in its new BlueMotion Technology. BlueMotion was a new innovation launched in European cars with the goal of reducing environmental impact without compromising on performance or the joy of driving.

> It's not the cost of The Unexpected, but the meaning

Volkswagen's campaign was based on the notion that making something fun would change human behavior for the better. It ultimately became known as The Fun Theory.

To test the theory that doing good could be fun — and enhance Volkswagen's brand along the way — they created three public initiatives: The Piano Stairs, Bottle Bank Arcade and World's Deepest Bin.

Each initiative was built around a single question, such as "Can we get more people to use the stairs by making it fun to do?"

The tests were documented, recorded and turned into a viral campaign shared on YouTube. The results were far beyond anything Volkswagen anticipated.

Piano Stairs

To create the Piano Stairs experiment, a single staircase in a busy metro station was turned into a living piano. Team members rigged the stairs to play a tune as people walked up or down it, encouraging them to interact with the staircase. At the same time, the additional behavioral goal was to discourage people from using the adjacent escalator, or even the nearby elevator.

From the moment people noticed that the stairs looked like piano keys, curious commuters and travelers started to try them. It didn't take long before the curiosity became a game — people began to jump from stair to stair just to see what kind of music they could make. And as the experiment wore on, it became more and more like the scene in the movie "Big," where actors Tom Hanks and Robert Loggia play a duet in the middle of FAO Schwarz by dancing and jumping on a large piano spread across the floor.

By the end of the Piano Stairs experiment, 66 percent more people chose the stairs than normal — and a viral legend was born across Europe.

Bottle Bank Arcade

For its second experiment, Volkswagen set out to get more people to use a bottle bank to recycle empty bottles. As with the initial experiment, this theory tied back to the carmaker's new "green" auto innovation. This question: Can fun change behavior for the better?

The Bottle Bank Arcade turned recycling into an old-school arcade game. A standard recycling container was retrofitted with electronics. When people threw bottles into it, the bank lit up and racked up points. Once more, it was unexpected ... and fun.

Over a single evening, Volkswagen's Bottle Bank Arcade was used by nearly 100 people. During the same period, the nearby conventional bottle bank had two users. Making it fun worked.

World's Deepest Bin

In its final planned experiment, Volkswagen pondered the idea of whether they could get more people to throw rubbish in a bin if they made it fun to do. They created what was called the World's Deepest Bin, and rigged the bin with an amusing cartoon-like sound of something dropping deep into the earth.

During one day, 72 kilograms of rubbish was collected. That was 41 kilograms more than the normal rubbish bin during the same time period.

Looking at these three experiments in delivering The Unexpected by making the experience fun, perhaps the most relevant pattern is that of emotional or affective engagement. Each experience was designed to evoke an emotional response and to motivate engagement through enjoyment, surprise or delight — key elements of The Unexpected.

The experiences were memorable and distinguishable. They were chronicled in such a way that they went viral. And then, because of the success of the first three initiatives, Volkswagen took it one step further and launched a public competition tied to promotions around its new cars. The auto maker challenged consumers to submit their own ideas on how to make doing the right thing more fun.

Among myriad ideas submitted was one that was selected and tested in Sweden — the Speed Camera Lottery, which to Volkswagen made sense because it was directly associated with driving cars on the road.

Speed Camera Lottery

For the Speed Camera Lottery, Volkswagen partnered with Swedish authorities to complement their already-in-place speeding patrols. A normal speed camera was used to document all drivers who were driving on a stretch of highway under the speed limit.

Using money collected from speeding fines, Volkswagen then helped set up a lottery where a portion of the money collected by the authorities was given to a random person who drove past the camera below the speed limit.

The test results were astounding: The number of people speeding on that particular road dropped by 15 percent. And, not only was this good for improving safety among drivers, the passionate approach was understandably good for Volkswagen's business as well. Market share in the eco market rose from 8 percent to 14.7 percent for Volkswagen, an 87 percent increase. Sales of its Passat EcoFuel rose by 106 percent. Overall, Volkswagen Sweden raised its share of the auto market from 10 percent to 13 percent, proving that making something fun was good for business.

Beyond the tangible benefits, the campaign also enhanced Volkswagen's global visibility and helped it build its green car line across Europe. At its core, the effort was a signature case of how effectively plying The Unexpected can have multiple positive effects on a business.

"If you work just for money, you'll never make it, but if you love what you're doing and you always put the customer first, success will be yours."
—Ray Kroc, founder, McDonald's

Similar results occurred for Coca-Cola, which since 2010 has developed unexpected experiences in more than 15 countries and on 10 U.S. college campuses through its Happiness Machine. A Happiness Machine also made a brief surprise appearance at the World of Coca-Cola from June to September 2012 at Pemberton Place, adjacent to the Georgia Aquarium in downtown Atlanta.

What is a Happiness Machine?

Well, at first glance it's a seemingly ordinary Coca-Cola vending machine. But when it's used the machine delivers spontaneous surprises to unsuspecting and randomly selected consumers.

The global beverage giant launched the idea on college campuses back in 2010 as part of a plan to share a little happiness with the student body. Students put coins and bills into the machine and were met with surprise and delight instead of just a standard can or bottle of Coke. In many cases, the back of the Happiness Machine was specially made and kept open, so that an employee could hide inside and distribute items that were far larger than anything that could have easily fit inside a standard vending machine.

Students fed the machine and were rewarded with handfuls of Coca-Colas — sometimes two, three, four or even five cans — as well as such items as bouquets of flowers, pizzas and even giant submarine sandwiches. The machines also were designed to entertain and draw attention. They lit up, made enticing sounds, and drew crowds of people who stood around waiting to see what would happen next.

"Where will happiness strike next?" instantly became the initiative's catchy tag line.

As news of Happiness Machine sightings on college campuses across the U.S. went viral, it not only raised awareness for Coca-Cola, but also created enormous buzz and anticipation about the machines.

In every case, hidden cameras filmed videos of the students' experiences, which when shared on YouTube quickly went viral. Millions of people watched.

Coca-Cola's timing couldn't have been better from a business standpoint. It launched the campaign during a time when sales had been slowing in the U.S. and globally. So while the campaign was designed to focus attention on Coke as a responsible — and fun — brand, it was also designed to spark sales.

It worked. Sales rose not long after the first videos hit the Internet and they have been gradually and sustainably rising ever since.

The Pemberton Place machine, which was the first machine in the U.S. to be placed outside a college campus, spent four months in one place — which was the longest time for any Happiness Machine to remain installed. It became part of the World Of Coca-Cola's global Summer Moments of Happiness promotion, and drew close to 100,000 guests who were treated to either a regular ice-cold Coca-Cola or walked away with one of nearly 4,000 summertime prizes, such as sporting goods, coolers and digital cameras — all in the name of summer fun.

In March 2014, Coca-Cola added a more humanistic element to its Happiness Machine campaign — and did so on a more global scale.

The company installed five special phone booths in Dubai labor camps that accepted Coca-Cola bottle caps instead of coins. In exchange for the cap from a bottle of Coke — which costs about fifty-four cents — migrant workers were able to make a three-minute international call.

Coca-Cola's concept was designed to draw attention to the lives of Dubai's migrant laborers, which are filled with hardship. Foreigners — including thousands of migrant workers from South Asia — make up more than 88 percent of residents of the United Arab Emirates, of which Dubai is a commercial and cultural center. The beverage maker's efforts were therefore aimed at that Asian and Middle Eastern market — and raising consumer awareness of what was going on.

In the ad, we learn that these workers make about $6 per day, and that it costs nearly a dollar per minute to call home — so phone calls are rare. Then the screen goes red with the company's brand colors, the music increases and a question is posed on the screen: So what if every Coke came with a few extra minutes of happiness?

We see laborers in hard hats and reflective vests lining up to use the machine — and grinning — as they wait to place a call. Coca-Cola says more than 40,000 people made calls.

Coke's Dubai ad was part of a series the company called Where Will Happiness Strike Next? It was developed to celebrate people having authentic experiences with Coke in which they're treated to The Unexpected.

In another ad, designed for the Singapore market, drones dropped boxes of Coke onto construction sites manned by migrant workers. The cans were wrapped in messages of appreciation from fellow Singaporeans. And, in yet another ad, this one designed for Bangladesh, people run across an arcade machine that runs on Coca-Cola empties.

Coke's efforts have proven successful. Each ad has attracted hundreds of thousands of views on YouTube — the Dubai ad, itself, has been seen by more than 1 million people across the globe.

When you think about it, making the experience fun can add a whole new dimension to delivering The Unexpected. There is little question that brands must develop ideas that consumers want to participate in, play with and pass along to others.

As with anything effective, the best ideas become sustainable and live well beyond initial exposure. In these instances, the viral component of The Unexpected comes into play. More important, people continue to talk about and build upon these ideas for years to come. In essence, they take on a life of their own.

Part Three

Building The Unexpected Organization

17 Have the Will to Succeed

When it comes to building an organization designed to perfectly deliver The Unexpected, one need look no further than Disney to find the role model. If you've ever been to a Disney property, you've experienced firsthand the magic delivered to visitors every day. You will never see surly employees shambling around Walt Disney World or Disneyland. You won't find litter scattered about the park, disrupting the experience. You will, however, be treated to a magical experience, be made to feel special during every encounter with team members and experience the unparalleled level of unexpected customer service that continues to stoke the Disney legend.

Disney achieves this experience without paying excessive premiums to its employees — yet clearly understands how important team member are and treats them thusly. Rather, Disney's ability to ply The Unexpected is the result of decades of meticulous planning and flawless execution.

Disney's leadership decided years ago that it would exercise an uncompromising will to deliver unexpected experiences, and religiously follow through with its plans. It strategically built delivery systems and designed elaborate training processes that teach new and existing team members what to do, how to do it and why. These systems are considered the industry gold standard and taught to other organizations across the globe.

The Internet brims with stories — and the shelves are filled with books — describing how the system works. At its core is training — priority No. 1 — and it, without a doubt, is the primary reason why Disney excels. In 1986, Disney took another step and founded the Disney Institute, which was designed to inspire and teach business professionals how to apply the best practices Disney perfected over its more than 80-year history to their own organizations.

These systems start with a rigorous hiring process and extensive continuous training. While complex for Disney's purposes, they don't need to be for other organizations to follow suit.

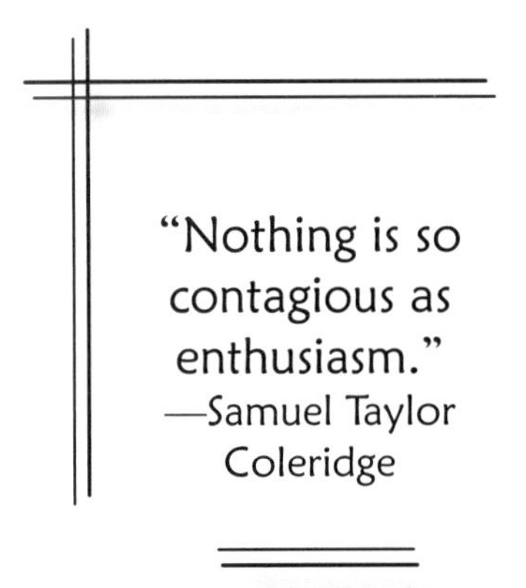

You do not need Disney's resources, its training manuals, or the decades of fine-tuning the process in order to effectively deliver The Unexpected in your organization. Instead, you must have the same will to succeed that Disney possesses. If you have an attitude that says, "We refuse to accept the status quo!" and if you've reached the conclusion that "good" isn't "good enough" for your customers, vendors and employees, you are already on the right path.

Still skeptical that you can duplicate the same type of results as The Mouse That Roars? Let's revisit the case of Veggie Grill, one of the fastest growing, regional restaurant chains in America. Based in California, Veggie Grill has been growing at an annual growth rate of more than 100 percent over the past few years and as of October 2014 had 26 locations across several states on the West Coast.

Veggie Grill has developed its own theories on The Unexpected and established highly effective methods to surprise and delight its customers when they least expect it. The chain has distinguished its brand from both national and regional competitors. It gets people talking. And it has become a profitable organization where price has become irrelevant. Simply put, it lives and breathes The Unexpected.

So how did Dollarhyde build an organization capable of delivering The Unexpected?

First, he and his management team hired like-minded people who saw service and providing a memorable experience as important as the food, itself. They empowered employees at every level to make front-line decisions when they saw opportunities to serve the customer. And, they invested in continuous staff service training.

Dollarhyde says this is crucial — the only way to ensure regular delivery of The Unexpected is by having the right culture staffed with employees who recognize not only when it's a good time to act, but are creative enough to think differently about what they will deliver. That's a delicate balance, he says, and one where larger companies often find themselves faltering.

"At a lot of the bigger restaurant chains, when they get bigger, they implement a lot of rules," Dollarhyde says. "And so the staff is not empowered to do unexpected things for their guests. They talk about empowerment, but there are times when they bog people down with paperwork after they deliver something that goes above and beyond — like free food or complementary drinks — so if you work there, you don't want to do it too often."

That potential flaw can create an unintended competitive advantage for organizations that have an entrepreneurial culture and a belief that The Unexpected can and will be used as a differentiator.

"Start with a system around your culture," Dollarhyde suggests. "That is your best plan — don't have a rigid series of rules and regulations. Instead, build a culture that says it's about enjoyment, customer enjoyment, and remember that it isn't just great food."

This system should include a well-thought-out series of events and actions that happen to a guest from the moment they arrive. Each must create that exceptional level of enjoyment, he says, which can then lead to "a whole range of unexpected experiences" as the opportunities begin to present themselves.

Additionally, Dollarhyde invests heavily in recruiting and training — it must be ongoing so that you have a continuous flow of people who keep buying into the program.

"You must get the right people or nothing else matters," he says. "They should be the type of people who will look you and the customer in the eye, are naturally smiling, have a history of achievement and are somewhat competitive. When it comes to finding ways to deliver unexpected experiences to customers, having people who are competitive makes it that much easier."

Then, empower your staff — at every level — to find ways to surprise and delight your customers.

"In the restaurant business, for example, you want people to eat items you're really proud of, so you encourage staff members to recommend those items to customers," Dollarhyde says. "But often, your customers are frugal, and if it's something that's outside the norm, they say 'no.'"

So Dollarhyde teaches his employees to give away free food, which on the surface may seem like a mistake when you're working in a thin-margin business.

"It's actually the opposite. For example, we're really proud of our carrot cake. It's really fantastic carrot cake," he says. "So if one of our servers suggests or recommends the carrot cake and the guest says, 'no,' we hope the server is observant enough to recognize whether it's because the guest doesn't want dessert or if it's because they don't want to 'buy' dessert."

Dollarhyde hires employees who see the difference. If it's the latter, delivering The Unexpected might mean having a waiter take it upon himself to return to the kitchen, get a piece of carrot cake and a couple of forks, and bring it out to the guest — at no charge — so that everyone at the table could taste it.

"That's The Unexpected for us," he says. "You surprise people when they least expect it. And then, when they leave the restaurant, they're saying to themselves and others, 'We have to go back there. I can't believe what they did for us — without even being asked.' But in order for that to work, our management team has to empower our staff not to think they're going to be in trouble for giving away food."

So how does this translate to any industry?

First and foremost, you must possess that will to get started and the wherewithal to follow through to the end — no matter how things shake out in the early going. Without your complete buy-in as senior management, any effort by your staff will be fruitless. They need to see that you're confident in the process and willing to let it evolve.

Earlier in the book, in Chapter 5, we explained what building blocks organizations must have in place to foster an organization capable of delivering The Unexpected. We can't stress these enough.

- Establish a servant culture where everyone is aligned with the mission of serving the customer.
- Empower people on the front line to identify opportunities to make creative and innovative decisions on how to deliver service to customers.
- Formalize systems capable of delivering surprise and delight.

These three steps rely on one bedrock principle: The right people working for you. That's non-negotiable. But, of course, it's often easier said than done.

To accomplish this, you must:

- Recruit and hire the best people.
- Invest in training so that you're developing a continuously resupplied army of like-minded team members.
- Maintain an unwavering commitment from your management team toward delivery of The Unexpected.
- Religiously follow whatever systems you develop and be willing to tinker with them until you get the system right.

And as you're doing this, you need to do four things:

1. Teach. Learn how to best explain to your team why delivering The Unexpected is important. Share the philosophy with everyone, thereby creating service fanatics who strive to outdo each other in order to provide the best and most memorable experiences. Remember, competition can be a good thing internally among your team members when it comes to effectively delivering The Unexpected.

2. Show. Remember what you learned in grade school — show don't tell. Provide concrete examples to your team members that illustrate how to recognize opportunities when delivering surprise and delight is possible and most appropriate. The greatest experiences often go viral and people can barely wait to share with others. It often begins with, "You won't believe what happened to me today ..."

3. Empower. Let the front-line employees make decisions about when and how to deliver The Unexpected to consumers — without interference or micromanagement from supervisors or higher-ups. These team members are on the front lines. They spend the most time with your customers and often know them much better than anyone else in your organization.

4. Reinforce. Share stories and acknowledge those people in your organization who deliver The Unexpected well. Create substantive recognition programs to reward people inside your organization who excel at it. And find ways to build the legend across your organization so that you're able to get your people excited about finding new ways to provide surprise and delight to your customers.

The most important ingredient, however, remains the one we've mentioned again and again — you need the right type of people on your team. They must be engaged and they must believe that delivering The Unexpected is an essential part of their core being. None of this will be sustainable unless your people buy into your vision for delivering The Unexpected and then make it their own.

There is a direct correlation between employee engagement and performance — this intersection is where people achieve their best results and, not surprisingly, are able to create the greatest experiences for your customers. It should therefore come as no surprise that this is also the point where your organization achieves its greatest potential — both in profitability and sustainable growth.

How do you get started building The Unexpected Organization?

First, start small. For example, if you have multiple locations, launch it in one place. Try unexpected gestures, surprise events, over and beyond services and totally unnecessary gifts.

Next, put some sort of system in place to measure the results. What's happening, and is it working? If so, why? If not, why not?

And then, once you've measured it, expand the initiatives that work. If it's viable in your San Francisco office, how can you make it effective in St. Louis? Does doing the same thing produce different results based on location? Or, are you finding it translates well everywhere?

Not surprisingly, this is a process. So you should continue to measure the results again and again. Did your adjustments work? If not, keep tweaking until you land on a formula for success. It's there. You may just have to keep looking and trying different combinations for a while until you find it.

Finally, don't forget that at its core, delivering The Unexpected is all about your people. So consider that the final piece of The Unexpected is your ability to deliver it internally to employees by building a culture that walks the talk. Simply put, if you want them to do it for others, you must first do it for them.

18 The Culture of The Unexpected for Employees

Part I — Above & Beyond

The over-commoditization of everyday products and services has produced widespread "low cost" provider wars across nearly every industry. You only need to look at the recent explosion in the dollar store industry to get a sense of what consumers are beginning to expect — an estimated $27.65 billion annually. This, in turn, has put even more emphasis on customer service as any organization's most important differentiator.

But what often gets lost in the conversation is that internal customer service is just as important — if not more so — than external customer service. If your goal is create memorable and distinguishable experiences for your customers, you better have your own house in order before expecting your workforce to create unexpected experiences outside its walls.

That means building a company culture engineered to think about The Unexpected every day, year-round.

We can't emphasize this enough: Everything comes down to your people. And if you want your people to deliver The Unexpected to your customers, vendors and constituents, you must deliver The Unexpected to them.

There are basically two ways you can do this — perks and recognition.

Perks refer to those unexpected above-and-beyond extras that your organization offers as part of its corporate culture, such as catered lunches or casual Fridays. Recognition can be something as simple as an Employee of the Year award or a handwritten thank you for an employee who went above and beyond for a client.

Further, there is a direct correlation among three common measures — company performance, reputation and employee satisfaction — and it's no coincidence that those who ply The Unexpected well excel in all three areas.

For example, among the top 25 organizations on *Fortune*'s 2014 Best Companies to Work For list, voluntary turnover among employees for calendar year 2013 was 9 percent. The national average that year was 10.4 percent. That's a 15 percent difference.

And while 15 percent may not seem like much, a closer examination of the actual cost to replace employees who voluntarily leave paints quite a different picture.

To replace a worker who earns less than $30,000 per year costs an organization about 16 percent of that person's annual salary — as much as $4,800.

Replacing a worker who earns between $30,000 and $75,000 annually, costs an organization about 20 percent of that worker's annual salary — between $6,000 and $15,000 per person.

And, replacing a highly educated worker in the executive ranks or specialty skill areas — typically those making in excess of $75,000 per year — carries an even higher price tag: As much as 213 percent of that person's annual salary. That means a $100,000-per-year employee could cost the organization as much as $213,000 to replace.

Suddenly, you're looking at a lot of replacement dollars that could be spent elsewhere — or better yet, dropped to your bottom line.

A similar story plays itself out in the financial performance of the public companies included on *Fortune*'s list: Google, Salesforce, Intuit, Camden Property Trust, Ultimate Software, NuStar Energy and Rackspace.

Combined, these unexpected organizations generated a 97.5 percent average increase in annual revenue and a 174.5 percent average increase in per share stock price over five years — providing value for both shareholders and the organization, alike.

Beyond the financial impact of higher turnover there are other factors at work — the loss of institutional knowledge, relationships and company morale. Those companies that keep that rate low maintain a powerful competitive intangible competitive advantage in those areas.

So what do these great places to work have in common that is different from other organizations? What do they — and other organizations that deliver The Unexpected internally to employees — do to ensure company cultures dedicated to providing memorable and distinguishable experiences for customers and vendors? More important, how do these organization go beyond providing world-class products and services that people need, want and buy?

Delivering The Unexpected internally enlivens your culture, builds loyalty and causes you're employees to say, "It's unbelievable what you do for me."

First and foremost, they focus on their employees. They know that if they deliver unexpected or special experiences to employees that they, in turn, will deliver The Unexpected to customers and vendors. Employees feed off each other, especially when they share success stories, and together raise the bar on both the experiences and the wow factor.

The most obvious way to achieve this is by building a well-trained workforce. Don't confuse this type of training with traditional on-the-job education. The best organizations incorporate unique training-related perks into their culture.

The Boston Consulting Group, No. 3 on *Fortune's* list, pays full tuition — including living expenses — for employees attending graduate school; Edward Jones (No. 4) provides a training program for veterans transitioning to a civilian career with a guaranteed salary for the first 12 months on the job; and for the first 30 days on the job at Intuit (No. 8), some departments offer a "no work, no worries" policy that allows new hires to familiarize themselves with how things work before jumping into their first true assignment.

Creating The Unexpected Perk for employees is happening in organizations large and small across the globe. And in some companies, professional and personal development opportunities are intertwined in completely unexpected ways.

At BBMG, a global brand innovation company based in New York City, employees are granted two separate accounts — one for "inspiration" and another for "professional development."

The company deposits $500 annually in each account for the employee to use as they like.

Employees' professional development accounts must be used on something specific to each employee's job title, such as attending seminars or taking courses. The inspiration account has only one criterion — personal growth, which could be something exotic like skydiving lessons, adventurous such as a backpacking course, or even artsy-crafty like a pottery class.

At Ruby Receptionists, every employee is given a five-week paid sabbatical that offers them a chance to pursue a dream or activity that makes him or her deeply happy. Ruby also provides each employee with a $1,000 grant to help.

Over the years, employees have filmed documentaries and visited foreign cities like Paris. One even fostered a daughter's dream of becoming a marine biologist by road tripping to numerous aquariums across the country.

Google, No. 1 on *Fortune*'s 2014 list, touts a laundry list of perks for employees, every employee receives up to $12,000 in tuition reimbursement per year — as long as they earn at least a "B" in all of their courses.

Google has conducted extensive research on the perks it offers and been able to measure comparable returns on investment for each. Prasad Setty, Google's vice president of People Analytics, and Laszlo Bock, the company's senior vice president of People Operations oversee the company's initiatives. Setty's team enables all people decisions at Google to be data-driven and generates detailed insight on how to best keep Googlers happy and productive. Bock leads Google's people functions and is responsible for attracting, developing, retaining and delighting Googlers — which effectively means putting Setty's theories into practice.

Here's one example: Google's revamped paid time off policy for new mothers.

Setty's research found that women were leaving the company at twice the rate of men, and it often occurred with new mothers. At the time, Google's maternity policy offered employees 12 weeks of paid time off. So Bock took that information and changed the plan, providing new mothers with five months paid time off, with full pay and benefits.

The result?

A 50-percent reduction in attrition for new mothers.

Another revelation Setty's research uncovered was that the way new employees were greeted had a profound effect on his or her initial productivity. By changing the words used — and ensuring they were delivered genuinely — Bock engineered a different warm greeting for new employees and a significantly positive result.

When a manager greets a new employee he says something akin to "Hi. Nice to meet you. You're on my team and we're going to be working together and doing a few other things."

This change to how employees were initially welcomed — alone — has translated into a measurable 15-percent increase in productivity from the employee over the following nine months.

It shouldn't be surprising when you consider Maslow's hierarchy of human needs. After physiological and safety needs are fulfilled, the third level of human needs is interpersonal, involving feelings of belongingness. Google's warm greeting to new team members delivers an immediate sense of belonging.

Consider the internal perks provided to employees at JANCOA Janitorial Services, a growing janitorial services firm based in greater Cincinnati.

Cleaning toilets and mopping lobbies is not sexy work — and JANCOA's management team knows this. In the late 1990s, JANCOA was struggling with high turnover. Staffing shifts had become a daily firefight, and the company's management team was hiring upwards of 50 people each week in hopes of having enough people to clean their clients' buildings each evening.

Despite this, JANCOA managed to fulfill its commitments.

But losing people every day, combined with the seemingly endless cycle of recruit-hire-train, was taking its toll on the company, its executives and the loyal janitors who were showing up to work their shifts.

JANCOA CEO Mary Miller was drained. She knew she had a people problem and decided to find a new approach to the solution. Instead of hiring more bodies and playing the attrition numbers game, Miller did something completely unexpected: She change the question from "How can we get more janitors?" to "How can we become the company that janitors want to work for?"

"I recognized that people are the engine of any company," Miller explains. "They drive an organization and they are ultimately responsible for our success or failure."

Deeply rooted in positive psychology, JANCOA's solution was a game-changer — transform the company from a janitorial services business into one that served janitors and clients. It was a long shot, but Miller believed the company had little to lose by trying it.

She and her team put their focus on employees. They recognized that if JANCOA was going to be successful, it would be because it was filled with teams of happy, satisfied employees who couldn't wait to do their jobs.

JANCOA developed a program called The Dream Manager, which was designed to work with every employee to help them achieve a specific life goal. Whatever goal the employee had — learning English, buying a home, paying for college — JANCOA pledged to help them achieve it. And Miller created a new position within the company, the Dream Manager, to oversee her promise.

"JANCOA began a mission to build a culture of dreams," Miller says. "We decided to work with our employees to help them build better lives, the lives they wanted."

When the program launched, JANCOA employees, eager to take advantage of the opportunity, quickly filled the Dream Manager's calendar. As word spread about the program, retention improved, from 107 percent turnover in one 90-day period to well below the industry average, as well as a near-zero absenteeism rate.

For the large number of Spanish-speaking employees, JANCOA brought in English teachers and hosted classes in their offices. For an employee who wanted to buy a home, JANCOA's Dream Manager helped her establish a savings plan and connected her to a lending agency and a real estate agent who had listings in her price range. Within six months of her meeting with the Dream Manager, this employee was moving into her new home.

What was truly unexpected, however, was the ripple effect JANCOA's innovative retention program had. Now, employees and former employees were referring friends for jobs. And employees who utilized the services of the Dream Manager began looking for ways to give back.

For example, when the employee who was able to buy her first home through the Dream Manager program learned another employee was sending her paychecks home to her family in Guatemala, she launched a canned food drive during the holidays in her client buildings to help the family.

The Dream Manager went viral. Groups began contacting Miller to learn more about the innovative program and see how they could incorporate it into their own organizations.

JANCOA's program inspired a best-selling book, "The Dream Manager," by Matthew Kelly (Hyperion, 2007). It took hold worldwide. Today, Chicago-based Floyd Consulting trains organizations on how to implement their own program and sponsors an annual Dream Manager award. The 2010 winner was even an international IT firm from South Africa, Netsurit.

All this was born from an unexpected perk the leader of a small family business had in hopes of improving its employee turnover rate.

At its core, delivering The Unexpected to employees means providing them with unique perks that they can't — and won't — get anywhere else. It motivates them to think about the end customer and ways they can delight them. And it keeps them engaged with the organization they work for — and its mission.

Among the more common-yet-unexpected perks companies nationwide offer are such things as:

- Happy hours and Beer Fridays.
- Pool tables and video games in the conference room.
- Ice cream sundae bars.
- Company-sponsored after-hours activities, such as trips to baseball games, concerts and bowling alleys.
- Monthly gatherings at local restaurants or bars to socialize with fellow employees.
- Free snacks and free beer on tap.
- Complimentary company branded T-shirts, mugs and blankets.
- Discounted gym memberships and health-and-wellness stipends.

- Employee discounts on company products and services.
- Fantasy football and March Madness tournaments.

Several of the organizations on *Fortune's* 2014 Best Companies to Work For list provided even more unexpected perks.

- SAS (No. 2) offers free breakfast every morning and an on-site massage therapist.
- The Boston Consulting Group (No. 3) lends new hires up to $100,000 as a down payment on a house.
- Quicken Loans (No. 5) encourages employee to dress up at work throughout the year for various themes, such as Dress Like a President Day, Worst Tie Day, Christmas in July, My Favorite College Day, 50s Day and Hawaiian Day. The mortgage lender also holds in-office sporting tournaments.
- Genentech (No. 6) holds Ho-Hos, a Genentech tradition, which are bimonthly company get-togethers every other Friday afternoon at rotating locations. The events have ranged from casual beer outings to parties to excursions at indoor ice rinks — each completely unique. Ho-Hos are designed to allow employees to unwind and become better connected with colleagues.
- Intuit (No. 8) hosts Idea Jams, where employees get four hours a week to work on pet projects that do not have to be directly related to their job. Between 2001 and 2013, Idea Jams helped Intuit generate $100 million in revenue. Additionally, on long days, Intuit teams can participate in 15-minute stretching, strengthening, or relaxation sessions that combine yoga, breathing and meditation.

"I have always believed that the way you treat your employees is the way they will treat your customers, and that people flourish when they are praised."
—Sir Richard Branson

- Robert W. Baird & Co. (No. 9) sends a bouquet of flowers or a gift basket to the homes of new hires.

Many top employers — and numerous others we researched — encourage employees to take time off to volunteer in their community (sometimes as many as 40 hours per year). Others matched employees' charitable donations. But Minnesota-based Orion Associates delivers an even more creative approach: It ties these things to training and the company's mission — and measures the results.

Orion CEO Dr. Rebecca Thomley recognized that service was at the core of what team members must deliver to its clients. Orion is a management company that specializes in social services support, primarily for nonprofits and NGOs, such as the Headwaters Relief Organization, a group that provides disaster relief. Thomley transformed what could have been run-of-the-mill training into an unexpected perk.

Thomley, who is an EY Entrepreneurial Winning Women™ 2011 Awards honoree, believes that proper training can mean the difference between significantly changing someone's life and simply providing a basic support system to a person in need. She acknowledges that there's a subtle difference between the two, but it's an important one.

To achieve her goal, Thomley determined that the best way to teach employees how to identify the greatest number of opportunities to deliver The Unexpected to others was by asking her team members to engage in as much volunteer work with different nonprofit organizations as possible — and to do so on company time.

"Orion has provided its employees with opportunities for creativity and self-expression through volunteerism," Thomley explains. "We have found that while we are helping others and building community, there are many benefits for the organization from the skills being developed."

The company provides this perk in the form of paid time off to pursue these initiatives, which Thomley says also leads to more passionate team members.

In 2009, Orion formally set the goal of 90 percent of its employees engaging in volunteer activities in service to their community. In response, Orion employees volunteered at the rate of 90.5 percent in 2009, 92 percent in 2010, 97 percent in 2011, and 100 percent in 2012, 2013 and 2014.

It's no accident that the closer you look at organizations that lead by example — providing unexpected perks to employees first — the more successful you find that these organizations are.

- Facebook offers new or expecting parents four months paid parental leave, reimbursement for daycare and adoption fees, and $4,000 baby cash for the new arrival. The company also provides free laundry and dry cleaning services.
- Google has heated swimming pools, offers employees on-site oil changes, bike repair, free health and dental appointments, nap pods and on-site physicians. They also have an on-site hair stylist.
- Zynga holds a monthly, company-hosted poker tournament.
- Cisco provides free tune-ups and oil changes for employees.
- Microsoft has its own shopping mall complex, which includes shops, a pub, soccer field and more than a dozen restaurants.
- Timberland gives a $3,000 subsidy to employees who buy a hybrid car.
- Ben & Jerry's employees can take three pints of ice cream home with them each day. They also get free health club memberships.
- LaSalle Network gives flowers to female employees on Valentine's Day and handwritten notes to all the mothers of employees on Mother's Day. The company holds monthly cooking competitions, including a chili cook-off.
- S.C. Johnson & Son offers concierge services that send packages, picks up groceries, take your car in for service, stand in line for concert tickets, shop around for the best deals on car insurances and pretty much anything you can think of, for employees.
- StumbleUpon caters lunch every day and offers $100 Uber car credits to each employee every month.
- Tumblr provides free car service for employees who work late nights.
- Eventbrite holds yoga classes and offers employees a never-ending snack supply.

- Airbnb gives $2,000 a year to employees so they can travel anywhere in the world. They also hold Formal Fridays — where everyone dresses up in their best clothes.

Clif Bar offers employees who commute to work on foot, bike, use public transportation or travel in carpools up to $960 a year. It also offers Cool Home Incentives, where employees can earn $1,000 a year to make economy-friendly home improvements, like Energy Star appliances, solar panels and energy-efficient windows. They also have a full-service gym, personal trainers, massage therapists and a chiropractor, as well as nutritional counselors.

You don't need to be a well-known brand — with deep pockets — to effectively deliver unexpected perks to employees.

- Kiva provides a monthly 30-minute recess for employees to eat free food, listen to music and play around in the office.
- Tagged holds monthly wine tastings.
- Asana gives each employee $10,000 to spend on office set up.
- Acuity has an on-site garden where employees can sign up to tend their own vegetable plots.
- At Threadless, you will find employees firing toy potato guns in the office at plastic parachute guys.
- SixthMan creates luxury travel events for employees where they can go on a cruise with their favorite bands.

Then there is a quiet little mailing and print services company in Nashville, Tennessee, that has garnered headlines for The Unexpected Perks it offers its employees.

By the time CEO Sherry Stewart Deutschmann was an EY Entrepreneurial Winning Women™ 2009 Awards honoree, she had already achieved widespread media attention for the culture she had built and growth she had attained at LetterLogic: The company had been named a three-time *Inc. 500* winner; recognized by *Entrepreneur* three times as one of the 50 fastest-growing women-led businesses in the nation; and its unique culture has been lauded by *Success*.

Deutschmann's culture instills a passion for going above and beyond in LetterLogic's employees, who strive to find creative ways to deliver The Unexpected to clients, day in and day out.

"We don't put the customer first," Deutschmann says. "We tell the customers that from the very beginning. We are putting the employees first, with the thought that if we took extraordinary care of the employees that they, in turn, would take extraordinary care of the customer."

While any organization can occasionally deliver The Unexpected, it is only those organizations that have fully developed their cultures and empowered employees to stretch their imaginations that are able to succeed on an entirely different level. LetterLogic is one of those rare organizations.

The company's culture has many branches, but it's safe to say it begins with its innovative profit-sharing program. From the company's earliest days, in 2002, LetterLogic has distributed 10 percent of its profits to employees, and that money is paid out monthly.

That, in itself, isn't completely unexpected. What is, however, is that the money is distributed evenly.

"The receptionist gets the same amount that the CEO gets," Deutschmann says. "And the CEO gets the same amount as the truck driver. It's a profit-sharing system that lets everybody know that their job is just an important as every other job in the company in order to get out a perfect product."

Additionally, the company pays 100 percent of each employee's medical, dental and life insurance. It also lets everybody bring their children and pets to work whenever they desire.

Employees are paid by the mile if they walk or bike to work.

"That's part of our greening initiative," Deutschmann explains. "But it's also to encourage employees to use public transportation. Each employee's ID badge is equipped with a public transportation pass so they can take public transportation at no cost anytime they want to go somewhere."

Deutschmann recognized long ago that happy and motivated employees would view the company as a part of their own family. In turn, they would go that extra step to deliver memorable and distinguishable experiences to customers. That would help generate extraordinary word-of-mouth referrals, which subsequently would grow LetterLogic's profits — essentially, The Unexpected in action.

"We help employees buy their first home with gifts for the closing costs or down payments," Deutschmann says. "If you have an entrepreneurial bone in your body, you can move from job to job in the company and learn about different areas. And when you're ready to leave, we will invest in your business."

LetterLogic even has a mistake quota.

"Everybody is required to come to the quarterly meeting explaining and publicizing their biggest mistake of the quarter and what they learned from it," she says. "You start to build trust and respect for each other when you're not afraid to expose your mistakes."

Deutschmann says all of this reinforces the company's motto, which is displayed on the walls of her company's office: "The Status Quo Sucks."

When visitors see it, they are surprised — adding yet another unexpected element to in-person interactions with LetterLogic and its team members.

"I think that is what has driven me," she says. "It's never quite good enough. I'm always looking for ways to improve, and I'm always challenging our employees to do things differently. When you do that, you find amazing things happen. And your customers will always be surprised."

19 The Culture of The Unexpected for Employees

Part II — Recognition

The final piece of building a culture that delivers The Unexpected to employees is creatively recognizing employees who deliver it internally and externally. Recognition fulfills another of Maslow's hierarchy of human needs — the need to be appreciated. By delivering unexpected recognition to employees, you're able to provide that psychological need.

Today, everybody expects two things from employers: good wages and health care benefits. But it's when you add a third component — The Unexpected — that you're able to build up the perception and reality of a great company. That's because companies that deliver unexpected recognition for employees create an aura about themselves. That aura in turn leads to stories people tell about working there, which then results in the reality of becoming a true employer of choice.

It's important to understand that in order to be unexpected, recognition can't be randomly — or too commonly — dispensed. It must be tied to something that merits it. Too often, we've allowed ourselves to become a culture where everyone receives a trophy or a pat on the back just for showing up and participating. This dilutes the power and impact of recognition and creates an unjustified feeling of entitlement. So it is imperative to make recognition as special — and unexpected — as the acts for which it is given.

When are relevant times to recognize employees? Examples may include:

- Accomplishing or exceeding a goal.
- Achieving an outstanding result.
- Demonstrating core values or teamwork.
- Enhancing quality.
- Going above and beyond.
- Helping a co-worker (at work or off-site).
- Increasing productivity.
- Improving efficiency.
- Providing exceptional contributions to organization.
- Delivering unexpected customer service to clients.
- Stepping up as a leader.
- Offering community service.
- Mentoring.

Companies with strong capabilities and competencies for delivering customer experience excellence traditionally outperform their competition.

It's important to think about how recognition is delivered to employees, as well as what type of recognition to employ. The most memorable and distinguishable recognitions work best.

Recognition should come from managers, not the HR department. A 2013 survey from Glassdoor, an online career site, reinforced this notion. It also revealed that the most effective recognition isn't part of a planned regular annual event or anniversary.

Peer-to-peer recognition can also be highly effective. Any easy way to do this is through nominations submitted by peers and then distributed by peers using company money or supported by the company and its management team.

Recognition in public has greater effect than one-on-one recognition. This public recognition can be done through mentions in company and client newsletters, through local and national media, social media announcements, at staff and department meetings, intranets, videos, bulletin boards, presentations.

Exam Coordinators Network, a Florida-based company that helps employers manage medical claims cases, uses an innovative ticket system, where employers and managers are able to give co-workers tickets for going above and beyond in the most creative ways with clients and fellow co-workers. Employees who receive tickets are entered into drawings for prizes at monthly town-hall-style company meetings.

At these meetings, each department is required to share stories about how they are helping clients, assisting employees, or otherwise surprising people in ways that makes ECN memorable and distinguishable, as well as a company of choice.

"The entire organization leaves with a better understanding of each department's role and how they're impacting people's lives by surprising them," explains Barbara Levine, the company's CEO. "They come away challenging each other to find new ways to do this."

By empowering front-line employees, Levine has built an organization of people who can deliver The Unexpected for ECN clients when they see it makes sense. "Our employees can problem solve and be engaged in the process by bringing their own unique personal strengths to the situation at hand," Levine says. "This also directly impacts job satisfaction because when you touch a customer directly you have the opportunity to surprise them and bring a little joy to someone's day."

The best recognition occasions are in the moment and are truly "surprises." The most innovative corporate cultures are about relieving stress and breaking down personal barriers so people can work as a team more effectively. Unusual, unexpected perks and constantly changing, creative rewards and occasions keeps employees happy, loyal and involved.

Consider this unexpected moment for an employee that happened in the fall of 2011, when retained executive search firm Howard & O'Brien

Associates decided to recognize the first full-time five-year employee in its brief corporate history.

Since its inception, Howard & O'Brien Associates sought ways to reward clients and the executives they place through small, thoughtful gifts. In every instance, team members looked to personalize the gifts to match the recipients. So when the opportunity to do something memorable for one of their colleagues arose, the leadership team seized the moment.

First, they planned a special dinner for the employee to celebrate her anniversary. They shared stories during dinner about the employee and the contributions she had made to the firm and its clients.

Then, at the apex of conversation, a window curtain at the restaurant was drawn open and everyone's attention shifted outside. Beyond the window, outside, in full view, was a silver Cadillac with a red bow.

Admittedly, not every organization can deliver The Unexpected by giving away a car. Giving someone a car certainly etches that experience in people's minds forever, and it does make for a great legend to be disseminated. There's nothing quite like having people look at you and say, "I wonder what they're going to do next?" But in the traditional business-to-business realm, delivering The Unexpected can just as easily come from small gestures, and occur in the most unexpected of industries. Not every organization needs to stretch to that level in order to do something memorable and distinguishable for employees. Simple, inexpensive things can work successfully, as well as lavish gifts.

CHG Healthcare Services (No. 16 on *Fortune*'s 2014 list), for example, distributes monthly $100 gift cards to six employees who are nominated by their peers. The gift cards are given with a personal card and visit from the CEO. And Acuity annually publishes a Top 100 Accomplishments list, which credits all employees involved.

Glassdoor's study showed that unexpected treats and rewards, like snacks, lunches and dinners, were the top form of non-monetary appreciation. Keeping it unexpected was crucial — creativity made the difference. While regular business meals — such as catering in lunch every

Monday — are a great perk, they aren't unexpected. To mix things up, consider surprising the office with an unexpected team breakfast in the middle of the week — or even smoothies for everyone in the middle of the afternoon.

It's important to keep recognition from becoming an entitlement. Once that happens, it's less of a reward. Regular weekly lunches turn into a perk instead. There's nothing wrong with this, but there is a distinct difference between perks and unexpected rewards.

And, instead of financial rewards, try to make a memorable impact on your team members by considering experiential ideas such as:

- ***Personal Services***: Gift housekeeping services or a personal chef visit at an employee's home for a customized one-of-a-kind meal for them and their family.
- ***Entertainment***: Tickets to the theater, the circus, a comedy show, a concert, a sporting event or a family-friendly event.
- ***Travel***: A bed and breakfast getaway weekend, plane tickets or a cruise.

You might consider putting up a thank you sign in the lobby with the employee's name on it and the reason why you're thanking them. You could arrange to have their car washed and detailed while they are working in the office.

Other ideas might be to recognize employees for delivering The Unexpected by offering to swap a task with them for a day or week — from the management level. You could have the entire team sign a framed photo or certificate of appreciation and present it to them in public. Give out an envelope stuffed with lottery tickets.

Then there are those who combine training with recognition — honoring those who get it.

With business customers located around the world, Global Payments counts on its customer service representatives to do more than simply solve client issues. The company provides electronic payment processing for credit cards, debit cards and check transactions for more than 1 million merchants worldwide, and pleasing customers by delivering unexpected moments is high on the company's priority list.

Global Payments accomplishes its goals through in-depth training for its call center employees — and subsequent recognition. The on-board program lasts six weeks. Focus is on the industry, internal systems and soft skills. New employees are taught the "why" as well as the "how." The training strategy is designed to build a team that recognizes what behaviors and actions most generate world-class customer service from the client's point of view. Customer service theory is combined with expert explanation and real-life over-the-shoulder-training — painting the bigger picture.

For those who get it, Global Payments provides generous rewards for living up to its standards. Recognition is viewed as "retention efforts" — further acknowledgement that Global Payments understands the power of creating memorable and distinguishable experiences for its clients.

Recognition includes Red Carpet Service or Beyond the Call cards, which are presented to call center agents after complimentary phone calls or emails are received. Positive emails are circulated companywide after a complimentary call is received. Peer awards, which are submitted by co-workers to recognize a peer who best exhibits the corporate values, are regularly presented. And Global Payments presents an Agent of the Month award to the individual who best demonstrates the ability to go above and beyond.

The results are increased profitability: 18 percent year-over-year growth. And it is in part because of a philosophy that starts at the top: Well-trained and empowered call center staff members engender brand loyalty and increased revenue through their delivery of The Unexpected. It doesn't get any clearer than that.

Some of the best ideas can be gleaned merely from talking to your peers that run other organizations or by visiting organizations that do it well. Bair had the unique opportunity to pick the brain of Zappos' CEO Tony Hsieh, who has become well-known for developing and fostering the company's unique culture.

After a tour of Zappos' home office in Las Vegas, Bair and her leadership team realized that any company's culture should be geared toward its mission and values, and that to be effective you need to use the talent of employees to create a fun culture.

So Bair decided to involve her entire staff in the development of Hobart's guiding principles (GPs) for the company to live by.

Today Hobart has seven GPs. This consortium of companies delivers strategic, account, medical and creative services — including database and market research, advertising and promotion, sales training, and contract and price management. No. 1 on the list is "Delivering quality, creativity and innovation to every client every day."

In order to accomplish this, every new hire is screened against the seven GPs. And performance reviews of existing staff members include benchmarking their performance against those seven GPs, "so that merit increases and bonuses are determined by how well our employees deliver The Unexpected to clients."

Explains Bair, "Our goal is to raise the bar by developing novel approaches to everything we do for the client — from status reports to account manager tools to the client meetings themselves."

"Businesses have to realize that providing excellent customer service is not an additional expense. It doesn't require hiring more people. It doesn't require any infrastructure. And it doesn't require any additional overhead. That's why it's a shame when places don't produce that excellent customer service." - Bryan Golden, author, *Dare to Live Without Limits*

One example of how Hobart recognizes employees for delivering memorable and distinguishable experiences for clients is the GP Wheel. Each month, employees whose tales of The Unexpected stand out earn the opportunity to spin the wheel and win a prize — which might be anything from a frozen turkey to a car wash to a new iPad. At the end of each year, all monthly winners pick from a bag of poker chips. Whoever pulls the gold chip spins the annual wheel, which offers prizes such as a big-screen TV or a dream vacation.

"It's something everyone looks forward to," says Bair. "And the video interview recaps we show with all the year's winners sharing the stories of what they've done for clients to earn recognition becomes quite effective in emphasizing that every employee has the opportunity to contribute, regardless of their position in the company. This really motivates the newcomers to keep their eyes and ears open for opportunities to deliver memorable experiences for clients and join the ranks of the winners."

Hobart also celebrates client wins in unexpected ways. One example was during 2012, when Bair's team executed a fake fire drill.

"We quietly donated money to the local fire department and asked them to bring in their trucks," she says. "The firemen, along with a group of Hobart employees, were dressed in full fire-fighting gear. They rushed in with the trucks, jumped out and ran into the building and announced that Hobart was officially 'on fire.' We surprised everyone and they loved it."

Not everyone has access to Hsieh, the author of "Delivering Happiness: A Path to Profits, Passion, and Purpose," but everyone can develop unique recognition programs and deliver The Unexpected to team members. There is even a nascent industry dedicated to helping employers do so. One is Snowfly, a full-service employee motivation and incentive company that offers a complete workforce incentives system that includes online programs, motivating rewards and consultative services.

Snowfly's incentive system allows companies to create, implement and manage their own incentive, recognition and reward programs, which are designed to engage and drive employee motivation. This is a great way to get the underlying structure in place.

It's important to remember that you can't lose the personal touch. Too many companies that choose to outsource their programs or turn it over to their HR department. Then they are surprised to find that it's not as effective as they anticipated. That's because coordinating recognition programs through a company's HR department more often than not results in it being impersonal rather than personal. Trying to deliver The Unexpected by design and through pre-programmed events also eliminates the element of surprise. And performance research backs this up, finding that a major reason recognition programs fail is that it gets outsourced to administrators rather than implemented and executed by managers who have real-life, day-to-day relationships with the employees they oversee.

The best organizations remember this. While they may outsource some programs to help them develop best-of-breed organizations, they ensure that the recognition remains personalized.

Another option is to use apps to help those delivering the recognition to both manage the programs and to keep them personal. iRecognize, a handy recognition assistant for managers developed by a company called Terryberry, can be used in conjunction with other programs. More important, it helps managers avoid the problem of allowing powerful recognition opportunities to fall through the cracks. Apps like iRecognize allow managers to do such things as send recognition instantly through Facebook, Twitter or text message; give appreciation e-cards to employees on the fly; keep a calendar for important recognition dates and reminders; and access recognition tools, checklists and resources for creative ideas.

There are also online or shared cloud-based systems that allow employees to recognize one another, earn points and recognition, as well as view who is being recognized and why they're being recognized throughout the organization — in real time.

Whatever you develop, it must be an integrated approach — and it doesn't have to be fancy, expensive or even technology-based.

At Firefighters Community Credit Union, based in Cleveland, simple works best. Being a credit union isn't sexy, but when 25,000 members count on you for their financial service needs, it really isn't about the sizzle. Rather, it's about the service you provide to ensure members' financial stability.

FCCU has no illusions about why it's in business and where its emphasis should be. With a 91 percent "A" service rating by its members, FCCU treats its members like family and constantly looks for ways to surprise and please them. And its leadership team knows that only happens when its employees are motivated to do so — and recognition is one way to ensure this.

In 2006, FCCU began developing systems designed to enhance its service value to its members. One of the programs launched internally to help achieve this goal was a quarterly Most Valuable Teammate (MVT) Award, which recognizes one staff member whose actions far exceeded the call of duty through a single interaction with a FCCU member or FCCU teammate.

One MVT is selected each quarter. The award recipient is honored with a PRIDE pin (FCCU's credo represents five key attributes expected of every team member — Professional, Respectful, Individuals, Devoted and Excellence) to attach to his or her Credo card, along with a gift valued at $100. This can be anything from a day at a sporting event to a Macy's shopping spree.

Winners are announced in the organization's quarterly newsletter and at FCCU's annual meeting. Even non-winners are feted through distribution of M.O.R.E. ribbons, which stands for the credit union's Mission to providing Outstanding service, Recognize service and Exemplify service.

Like FCCU and others who deliver unexpected recognition well, everything begins by hiring with an eye to creating the desired company culture. If you want a company filled with employees who compete to identify opportunities to deliver The Unexpected, you must hire like-minded people. Many companies even have a Fun Director or Chief Customer Experience Officer, whose job it is to think about ways to further engage the team. The best companies foster a healthy work/life balance — promoting personal growth and off-the-job activities as well as in-office or office-sponsored programs. And they recognize that employee independence pays off.

Finally, to become a highly effective organization that delivers The Unexpected for employees, don't forget these three key factors when considering recognition:

1. Make it personal. Design recognition to fit the recipient. If everyone gets the same gifts or gift cards you aren't thinking about the people involved and what they like. Not everyone likes the same restaurants, gift baskets or type of recognition. Effective recognition is also great for the recipient.

2. Be specific. Tie recognition to specific accomplishments. It lets people know you're paying attention to their performance and reviewing the results.

3. Spread it around. Don't just keep recognizing your top performers, even if they are expert practitioners of delivering The Unexpected. Expand the pool to recognize others on the team who are doing the little things that help contribute to delivering The Unexpected for your customers, and employ your superstars to help mentor others. The more people get recognized, the more being recognized becomes viral throughout your organization.

Remember, recognition can be a powerful tool to ensure delivery of The Unexpected. But it's just that — one more tool in your arsenal. If you learn how to use it wisely, your company, employees, vendors and customers will thank you for it.

20 Final Thoughts

Depending on your age, you might remember the days when every household waited for the new Montgomery Ward or Sears catalog to arrive; the corner drug store had the best soda fountain in town; and buying high-end clothing required a special trip to the tailor shop. Back then, being a retailer carried a certain prestige with it — often with higher profitability than other industries.

As recently as the very beginning of the 21st century everyone still had his or her own special niche:

- Grocery stores offered the freshest produce, choice meats and the widest selection of dairy products.
- CPA firms focused solely on audits and taxes.
- Pharmacies filled prescriptions, sold over-the-counter medication, carried health and beauty products, and had whatever you needed to fill your bathroom and medicine cabinet.
- Car dealerships sold cars while body shops and garages handled maintenance and repairs.
- Electronic stores sold TVs, stereos and consumer devices.
- Appliance stores sold refrigerators, washing machines and ovens.

Today, the rules of the game have changed. Lines that previously separated retailers have blurred — sometimes to the point of being indistinguishable. Chalk it up to the Amazon Effect.

First, let's be clear. The Amazon Effect isn't a bad thing. In fact, it's directly led to more innovation, faster adaptation and greater customer experiences. But the Amazon Effect is real, and it impacts anyone and everyone that considers themselves a retailer or service provider — online or offline.

> "Here is a simple but powerful rule: Always give people more than what they expect to get."
>
> —Nelson Boswell, author, *Inner Peace, Inner Power*

The Amazon Effect began innocently enough as what was then considered the Walmart Effect, starting with the explosion of big-box retailers back in the 1990s. Big boxes not only supplanted traditional department stores, but they also made available a much wider variety of products that previously could only be had at specialty stores.

But then, as consumers demanded lower prices and easier shopping experiences — i.e., the one-stop-shop — the largest of the big boxes, Walmart and Target, noticed and took action. They successfully expanded into such realms as grocery and pharmacy products and services, eye care, banking, medical care and even doing consumers' tax returns.

After the initial explosion of online retailers, the 800-pound gorilla known as Amazon evolved as well. Today, Amazon has become the dominant industry player, expanding well beyond its original roots of selling books and music and supplanting Walmart as the organization with the greatest impact on how consumer purchase goods and services. Today, you can buy pretty much everything and anything you want on Amazon — even food products. It isn't a stretch to predict that Amazon will soon branch out into connecting consumers and businesses with personal and professional service providers. In fact, in more than a dozen cities, Amazon already offers same-day delivery. And, in New York City, the company has started using bike messengers to experiment with one-hour delivery.

All of this has resulted in the stiff challenges everyone in business today faces. And, from what we saw along the way from the very public woes of such formerly well-known brands as Kmart, Lehman Brothers, Kodak, Blockbuster, E.F. Hutton, Borders, Pan Am, Arthur Andersen, Palm and CompUSA, the nasty fact is that economies of scale can no longer level the playing field.

Adapting through innovation — and adapting quickly — is really all that matters.

Service differentiation — specifically the ability to deliver memorable experiences, surprise and delight — has become the most effective way to protect an organization's long-term survival. Simply delivering world-class customer service is no longer enough to differentiate yourself from competitors. As we said near the beginning of this book, it's swiftly becoming your ante.

Looking deeper, several other factors currently are also at work. Among them:

- Notoriously low profit margins — in some industries less than 3 percent.
- Commoditization of products and services — with the largest companies setting what consumers consider "the acceptable price" for many items.
- Free shipping and aggressive pricing from online retailers, such as Amazon, and catalog companies, such as L.L. Bean, which has essentially eliminated any noticeable difference between shopping at home and shopping in a store.
- Stiff competition from online organizations — and those that use the Internet and social media to supplement their brick-and-mortar locations — all of which have figured out how to extend their reach beyond their own backyards.
- The proliferation of daily deal sites and instant online coupons.

There is little doubt that the increased pressure to innovate — online and in person — has produced both immediate and long-lasting effects on everyone in business. Expanding the product offering and lowering prices will only take you far. Long-term success will be rewarded to those organizations that can create the most memorable experiences and longest-lasting impressions. In simple terms, find unique ways to own your niche...and then scream it from the rafters.

One way is to implement public-facing programs that better brand who you are, define why people should choose you over the competition, and allow you to surprise your customers in nice ways when they least expect it

As we've discussed throughout this book, this process can be as simple as publicly recognizing your employees' above-and-beyond efforts to delight customers. Or, it can be as complex as employing big data to personalize every shopper's experience and surprise repeat customers so that you become their retailer-of-choice.

Not too long ago, it used to be enough to hang an Employee of the Month plaque at the front of a building to demonstrate that your organization put an emphasis on service. That's no longer either a differentiator or even unique.

Dare to be different by transforming your employee recognition into a public forum. Such transparency has never been as important as it is these days, especially in a world where privacy has taken a back seat to ease-of-use. Public recognition has the effect of making people notice you, and it can dramatically alter your company culture — especially when the recognition is based on your employees' ability to deliver memorable experiences at every possible public touch point with consumers.

Some of the more progressive companies in the world are even employing Chief Customer Officers, whose job it is to think about ways to provide unexpected delights to customers every day. This effort, along with other initiatives, is creating serious challenges to the status quo.

The use of big data has also become a key to differentiation as it continues to infiltrate our daily lives. Big data creates both positive and negative effects. You only need look as far as the massive data breaches at Target, Home Depot and dozens of other prominent businesses to recognize that we live in tricky times. But it is because of this increased level of information that we know so much about our customers and are able to innovate new ways to deliver surprises that we might have never considered before.

"Even the best of what formerly passed for good customer service is no longer enough."
—Gary Vaynerchuk, author, *The Thank You Economy*

Take for example a popular smartphone app called RetailMeNot, which bills itself as the world's largest digital coupon marketplace. The app allows consumers to find hundreds of thousands of digital coupons from myriad retailers and brands. RetailMeNot claims more than 16 million people have downloaded its app, which isn't surprising considering the popularity of daily deal sites and digital coupons.

But it's not the concept of digital coupons that provides The Unexpected for consumers who use RetailMeNot. Rather, it's the ability to personalize the app to recognize your favorite retailers and then synchronize those selections with your smartphone's GPS system.

While you're traveling around during the normal course of your day, RetailMeNot recognizes which brands you're near and generates instant notifications about personalized, special offers. For example, say you're near a Starbucks, RetailMeNot sends a quick message saying if you go in now, you can receive a free cup of coffee. Or, in case you weren't aware, there's a flash sale at Gap for 25 percent off of shorts and T-shirts that's good for the next few hours. RetailMeNot's power is based on its understanding that there are few things that can create more immediate delight than finding out that you can get something special now, without having to do much of anything extra.

All of these factors lead to a single conclusion: The old rules of market competition have started to become obsolete.

It used to be that in any one market, competition would weed out the weaker competitors and up to three organizations would end up the winners. Your goal was to compete hard enough and long enough to make the cut.

For example, when Circuit City went out of business, everybody thought Best Buy would own the market. When Linens 'n Things closed, conventional wisdom put the safe money on Bed Bath & Beyond. And when Borders failed, Barnes & Noble looked like the big winner. But the marketplace has continued to shift rapidly, and being the last man standing no longer ensures victory. The survivors have not benefited substantially by the reduced competition.

The bottom line is that things such as the Wal-Mart Effect do not have to be category killers. Rather, they are a new impetus to innovate, build a brand and find new ways to deliver The Unexpected.

If you want to win in this rapidly changing business world, providing great customer service is no longer enough. We are sprinting toward a world where delivering world-class service will be considered maintenance, not a differentiator. That, alone, should be reason for concern.

Two main factors are behind his paradigm shift.

First, we live in a crowded marketplace. There is more of everything today than what the consumer needs and has the disposable income to buy. The consumer world is quickly becoming over-stored and over-serviced. It's already here in the U.S. Just look at the retail sector and it's evident that we have a surplus of products and services: There are 40-square feet of retail space for every man, woman and child in the U.S. Compare this to Europe, where there are only 4-square feet for each person, and it's easy to see how difficult it is to stand out.

Because of over saturation, tomorrow's standout winners will be those people and organizations that are able to deliver The Unexpected —

unexpected products, unexpected services and unexpected experiences. By doing so, they will separate themselves from the pack.

Second, social media has made the world smaller and more connected. Today, we live by people telling other people how great — or terrible — things are. Our smartphones and mobile devices continually connect us, and we update our statuses in real time for everyone to see.

Competition has always been won by how well a product or service is noticed, referred or recommended. It is a simple equation: The more people that talk about it, the more business you get. But social media has rewritten the rules of engagement, and swiftly disappearing are the days where TV, radio and newsprint are the dominant media sources. While still influential, traditional media has already been regulated to second chair by social media, where stories are literally transmitted to the masses in milliseconds.

More important, the stories that people want to tell through social media are the stories of those people, places and things that are exceptional — stories that are unexpected. When it comes to business tales of The Unexpected, people can't wait to spread the word.

I began this book by recounting about an experience my colleagues and I had several years ago on JetBlue. Coincidentally, a similar experience happened in July 2014 on a Frontier Airlines flight that left Ronald Reagan Washington National Airport and was bound for Denver.

Bad weather in Denver forced the flight to circle in western Nebraska for long enough to cause the plane to run low on fuel. The plane was forced to land in Cheyenne, Wyoming. What happened next created one of those viral stories.

After spending more time than anticipated on the runway in Cheyenne — about an hour — Frontier Captain Gerhard Brandner determined everyone on the plane had not eaten in hours and took matters into his own hands.

Recalls Logan Marie Torres, a passenger who also was Miss Colorado United States Teen 2014, "He came over the intercom and said, 'Ladies and gentlemen, Frontier Airlines is known for being one of the cheapest airlines in the U.S., but your captain is not cheap. I just ordered pizza for the entire plane.'"

Brandner had called Dominos and ordered more than 50 pizzas to be delivered to the plane while it sat on the tarmac.

It has become very clear that your organization's ability to win will depend on your ability to deliver The Unexpected to your customers, vendors, prospects and employees. This skill, combined with empowering team members to employ creativity on the front line, will mean the difference between winning and losing.

Size no longer matters in this discussion. Deep pockets will not translate into easy victory. Small companies can deliver The Unexpected just as effectively as large organizations. In some ways, smaller companies might even have an advantage over their larger brethren because smaller companies typically have fewer hoops to jump through to get things done.

Fewer layers mean fewer rules and regulations. And fewer rules and regulations means it is easier to empower people on the front lines.

Nearly 9 out of every 10 U.S. consumers say they would pay more to ensure a superior customer experience.
Source: Customer Experience Impact Report, Harris Interactive/ RightNow)

Consumer demands are quickly shifting, and people are changing how they want to source their goods and services. Today more than ever, to win somebody must be exceptional. And it will only continue to accelerate into the future. Those who adapt to this new paradigm — no matter their size — will survive and thrive. Those who do not will fail.

And the way the winners will do this is simple and straightforward: They will deliver The Unexpected.

Final word: We invite you to deliver The Unexpected in your own organizations. Then share with us what you're doing, how it works and the results. The Unexpected is a living, breathing idea. It will continue to grow as people develop innovative and unique methods to implement and deliver it. We're interested in hearing about your experiences by writing to us at hbrodsky@ccaglobal.com or dsklein@sbnonline.com. As we continue to champion The Unexpected, we'll share your best ideas with others on The Unexpected blog at www.unexpectedthebook.com.

And so it begins.

About the Authors

Howard Brodsky is co-founder, chairman, and co-chief executive officer of CCA Global Partners, one of the largest privately held companies in the United States. CCA is comprised of 13 divisions with more than 3,000 locations worldwide and aggregated annual sales in excess of $10 billion. A pioneer of the cooperative business model, Howard has dedicated his career to helping entrepreneurs build successful businesses by applying his scalable business models to other industries. He is a member of the Entrepreneurial Hall of Fame, World Floor Covering Industry Hall of Fame, and National Cooperative Hall of Fame. He has been recognized as an Entrepreneur Of The Year by EY. He has been chairman of the National Judging Committee for the North American Entrepreneur Of The Year Program. Howard is an active speaker, civic leader, and well-regarded entrepreneur. He lives in Manchester, New Hampshire.

Dustin Scott Klein is an award-winning business journalist, bestselling author and the publisher of Smart Business magazine, a national chain of management journals for senior executives. Dustin is a former news reporter and business editor, as well as noted speaker on innovation, entrepreneurship and the art of storytelling. He has interviewed thousands of business leaders and helped more than a dozen CEOs and entrepreneurs transform their ideas into books, including as co-author of the Amazon #1 bestseller *The Benevolent Dictator*. He lives in Shaker Heights, Ohio, with his wife, Laura, and children, Sam, Cole and Mollie.